More praise for *The Credible Company*

"This is a book about people communicating *with* people, not communicating *at* them. It is about the message, not the medium. And it is about communication, analysis, reflection, and clear-thinking, not about speed of delivery, sound bites, and instant judgments. *The Credible Company* is the perfect sequel to D'Aprix's best-selling *Communicating for Change*."
—**Wilma Mathews,** Arizona State University

"Most business management books center on one simple concept; one chapter is often the whole premise. Roger's book is full of practical ideas and approaches to improving business today through effective communication. You'll want to read this whole book."
—**Karen Horn,** SVP, Corporate Communication, Washington Mutual

"The wisdom of a lifetime of experience, from the world's greatest internal communication guru, in one very easy-to-read volume. Compulsory and compulsive reading for everyone interested in improving organizational performance."
—**Rodney Gray,** Employee Communication & Surveys, Sydney

"Roger D'Aprix has once again put his finger on the pulse of business communication and developed a practical book to make companies credible with a skeptical workforce. His INFORMS model is elegant and is based on theory, research, and his extensive experience as a communication executive and consultant. This work will become an important part of both the scholarly literature and every business communicator's bookshelf. If you've ever felt that the concept of trust was too slippery to grab a hold of, grab a hold of this book."

—**Diane M. Gayeski,** PhD, associate dean and
professor of strategic communication,
Roy H. Park School of Communications
at Ithaca College

The Credible Company

The Credible Company

Communicating with Today's Skeptical Workforce

Roger D'Aprix

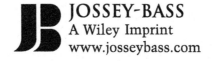
JOSSEY-BASS
A Wiley Imprint
www.josseybass.com

Published by Jossey-Bass
A Wiley Imprint
989 Market Street, San Francisco, CA 94103-1741—www.josseybass.com

Readers should be aware that Internet Web sites offered as citations and/or sources for further information may have changed or disappeared between the time this was written and when it is read.

Limit of Liability/Disclaimer of Warranty: While the publisher and author have used their best efforts in preparing this book, they make no representations or warranties with respect to the accuracy or completeness of the contents of this book and specifically disclaim any implied warranties of merchantability or fitness for a particular purpose. No warranty may be created or extended by sales representatives or written sales materials. The advice and strategies contained herein may not be suitable for your situation. You should consult with a professional where appropriate. Neither the publisher nor author shall be liable for any loss of profit or any other commercial damages, including but not limited to special, incidental, consequential, or other damages.

Jossey-Bass books and products are available through most bookstores. To contact Jossey-Bass directly call our Customer Care Department within the U.S. at 800-956-7739, outside the U.S. at 317-572-3986, or fax 317-572-4002.

Jossey-Bass also publishes its books in a variety of electronic formats. Some content that appears in print may not be available in electronic books.

Library of Congress Cataloging-in-Publication Data

D'Aprix, Roger M.
    The credible company : communicating with today's skeptical workforce /
    Roger D'Aprix.
        p.   cm.
    Includes bibliographical references and index.
    ISBN 978-0-470-27474-3 (cloth)
        1. Communication in personnel management.   2. Communication in management.
    I. Title.
    HF5549.5.C6D344   2009
    658.4'5—dc22
                                                                    2008027544

FIRST EDITION
HB Printing   10 9 8 7 6 5 4 3 2 1

Contents

Preface: Why This Book Is Important   ix

Prologue: From Entitlement to Capital Asset   xiii

1. A Morality Tale   1

2. Information   17

3. Needs on the Job   43

4. Face-to-Face   59

5. Openness   73

6. Research   87

7. Marketplace   105

8. Strategy   117

Epilogue: A Profession at a Crossroads   135

Notes   147

Acknowledgments   149

The Author   153

Index   155

For Theresa, my lifelong partner,
who has endured, indulged, and supported my work
since the first day we met . . . and for our seven grandchildren—
Matthew, Luke, Sarah, Joseph, Charley,
and the twins, Kate and Abigail

Preface

Why This Book Is Important

The first question any busy person should ask in browsing through a book like this one is: Is this important enough for me to spend my valuable time on, or should I search for a good novel instead? Let me try to answer that question and tell you the essential message of this book in four brief bullet points:

- Today's organizations are undergoing revolutionary change that has turned their relationship with their employees upside down.
- Those employees are increasingly skeptical, if not cynical, about the communication they receive at work.
- Because employees are now the *means* of doing business as opposed to their former status as the *cost* of doing business, the credible company is the one that takes note of the changed relationship and treats them like the precious asset they were always told they were—even when company actions often belied that claim.
- Company leaders and the communication professionals who are supposed to advise them had better understand the changed relationship and concoct communication strategies that are suited to these changed circumstances that, taken together, constitute a workplace revolution in an increasingly complex global economy.

With information the lifeblood of today's intellectual capital assembly line, the internal communication task has taken on unprecedented importance in the contemporary organization. Today's leadership is increasingly aware of the importance of educating its workforce to the realities of strategy, competition, and the needs of customers and shareholders. Without that education the workforce is left to guess about the organization's issues and its strategy to confront and resolve those issues. Because the worker is now a vital partner in that process, it is essential to ensure that he or she is fully informed.

The objective of this book is to analyze the critical elements of a communication strategy to reach a skeptical workforce. The reasons for that skepticism are many, including conducting massive downsizings over many years, taking for granted the contributions of talented employees, neglecting employee development and training, treating people as largely interchangeable, for the most part ignoring the all-important task of frontline leadership, and keeping people in the dark about future company intentions.

Whether you are a corporate leader, a communication professional charged with helping your leadership get through to a skeptical audience, or just someone interested in the dynamics of communication leadership, this book is worth your time and attention. If, on the other hand, you believe that communication is a simple matter of putting out a few facts, cranking up the company intranet, and letting the process take care of itself, you probably will be better off with that novel I alluded to earlier.

Who Should Read This Book—and How

Having said that, the question remains: who will benefit the most from this book? The potential audience is a broad one—anyone who cares about the process of helping people find greater meaning in their work and in making the workplace more productive and more honest. That should certainly include those colleagues of mine who make their living by producing credible communications for their coworkers. Or those aspirants who for one reason or another respond to that noble purpose of making our work the fulfilling venture we all desire but too rarely experience. Work has become our religion in the twenty-first century, for good or for ill. We are absorbed in it. We sacrifice our needs for it—and sometimes the needs of the people we care most about. And we long for the dignity and self-worth that it provides for us.

The leaders who carry the responsibility to make their organizations competitive and credible to the people they employ are also a natural audience for this book. In the end it is *their* responsibility to provide the kind of workplace culture in which people can flourish in the pursuit of worthwhile goals. In my view that is a vital—and maybe even a sacred—trust that cannot be delegated to anyone else.

If you disagree with that view and regard companies and other institutional organizations only as profit-making engines regardless of how they accomplish that goal, this book is also not for you. If, on the other hand, you see those institutional organizations as living products of our human need to unite our talents in pursuit of worthwhile goals, read on.

This book is organized so that the chapter titles create an acronym: INFORMS. That is an apt framework for a book that purports to be a prescription for effective communication. The prologue and the eight chapters that follow show the movement from employee entitlement to capital asset; an epilogue defines the challenges facing the communication profession in a global economy. Chapters Two through Eight contain the meat of the book: a prescription for those with the insight and motivation to work for greater credibility within companies and other institutional organizations.

Chapter Two talks about the changing nature and importance of information as a raw material for today's knowledge assembly line. Chapter Three focuses on the human needs that everyone brings daily to the workplace. Chapter Four highlights the critical role played by face-to-face communication, even—or more to the point, particularly—in a highly wired society. Chapter Five makes the case for greater openness and less secrecy in the workplace.

Chapter Six chiefly addresses the communication professionals who must conduct appropriate research as a foundation for their various strategies. Chapter Seven emphasizes the importance of turning all eyes outward to the marketplace as the source of and rationale for today's explosive change. And Chapter Eight shows how the INFORMS communication prescription finally comes together as a coherent strategy for greater company credibility.

The Credible Company is the product of a lifetime spent in appreciating and working with the dynamics of human organizations. It is a collection of my observations, opinions, and conclusions based on that lifetime of experience in determining how to communicate with a skeptical employee audience. As such it represents only my own views, which may or may not be shared by my talented colleagues at ROI Communication. If there are any errors, omissions, or lapses in logic, they are strictly my own responsibility.

I hope that *The Credible Company* will inspire its readers to see the nobility of this vital task of effective workplace communication as I see it. Welcome to the new and exciting world of internal communication in large organizations.

Roger D'Aprix
Rochester, New York
Fall 2008

Prologue

From Entitlement to Capital Asset

The employee audience in any large organization today is skeptical at best and cynical and turned off at worst. And they clearly have their reasons.

This level of employee disenchantment was not always so. When I went to work for General Electric in the early 1960s, as a young man interested in, among other things, how people adapted to working in large organizations, that task was relatively clear. In those days you generally went to work for a large company. You did your job as you understood it. And if you performed reasonably well and stayed out of trouble, you probably had a job for as long as the company was profitable. Layoffs were infrequent and almost always simply a result of unexpected downturns in company fortune.

American companies of that era, and well into the 1970s, practically owned the global marketplace. The reason was not always obvious to the American worker, but in retrospect it was pretty simple. The rest of the world was still recovering from the devastation of World War II. So American companies could pretty well operate on the presumption, "Here is our product; take it or leave it. It's all the same to us, because if you don't take it, someone else will." I oversimplify to make a point, but this is not too far off the mark for many American companies of that period.

In such a climate American corporate executives were willing, although sometimes with considerable resentment, to give the worker his way. The generous union agreements of that era are clear evidence of management's desire not to interrupt the revenue stream. Lifetime employment was not guaranteed, but it was certainly not uncommon for someone to come out of school, join a large organization, and retire with a solid pension some forty or so years later. In fact, so common was the experience that it gave rise to a sense of worker entitlement expressed bluntly at each contract bargaining session by the union rep and largely assumed by the professional workforce, who silently cheered on the union activists because their efforts would lead to benefits for all.

In this happy world, employee bands and choirs, semi-pro athletic teams, and all sorts of employee social arrangements were common. In Rochester, New York, where I live, Eastman Kodak (known for years by its employees as the Great Yellow Father) was noted for providing on each St. Patrick's Day a rich annual employee bonus that gladdened the hearts of local merchants. (Interestingly, even today, when Kodak is a shadow of its former self and continuing to lose money, the bonus remains. Only once, during the Depression, did Kodak fail to pay the wage bonus.) In earlier times Kodak also frequently brought in cut-rate employee entertainment by expensive Hollywood and Las Vegas performers to appear at the company theater for the pleasure of employees and their families.

Nor was Kodak unique in this form of employee largess. If you look at the archives of most large organizations of the day, you can easily find photos of company stores where products were sold at a deep discount, company golf courses, company picnic grounds, bands and choirs, traveling basketball teams, and similar employee activities and programs, all geared to attract and produce a satisfied workforce committed to the company as a kind of quasi extended family.

Were the employees of that day happier and less likely to express their distrust of and cynicism about management? For the most part, yes. It was a time of stability, presumed employee loyalty, and paternalism. I still recall the time when, as a young GE writer, I made a flip comment to my coworkers over coffee about some forgotten company practice, only to be taken aside by a kindly old gentleman named Brad, who had forty years or more of GE service. Gently but firmly he mentored me with the comment, "Young man, I resented your comment today. This company took care of me and my family in the depths of the Depression, and I'll never forget it. My advice is to keep those opinions to yourself." I haven't heard of or seen a similar episode in the last thirty years.

But that humbling experience aside, it was not surprising that people grew to feel entitled in such an environment. For example, I recall years later overhearing two Kodak women complain bitterly because Kodak had threatened to make the Kodak wage dividend bonus merit-based according to both individual and company performance. Until then it had been based only on the company's annual results in an era when better and better was the expectation and the reality.

Did all of this paternalism come with a price? Absolutely, because the expectation was that in return employees would be loyal, less resistant to change or unpleasant working conditions, and likely to stay for the long haul. Indeed, the so-called "job hopper" was anathema and likely to find himself looked on with deep suspicion. "Tell me, why have you had three jobs in the last ten years?" was the question posed by the uneasy corporate recruiters.

Change, Change, and More Change

Now fast-forward almost a half century to today's environment.

When I facilitate communication strategy workshops for professional communication staffers or for corporate leaders, I often begin with what I find to be an enlightening exercise. I ask the group to tell me what their companies are up against in their respective marketplaces. What, I ask, are the market forces that are shaping the strategies of your various companies? It's an interesting window into today's corporate America and its plight in a dog-eat-dog, globally competitive marketplace.

Here's a typical list of what these representatives of companies large and small and in every industry—from high tech to manufacturing to pharmaceuticals to utilities—say are the market forces that are determining the business strategies of their organizations:

- Globalization and the competitive pressures it's exerting
- The resulting intense cost pressures
- Demanding customers who want quality at ever-decreasing prices
- Technology that changes so rapidly it requires almost continuous learning to keep up
- Change, change, change, and more change
- Shifts from a manufacturing to a service to an information economy, with subsequent job displacement and creation
- Unrealistic shareholder demands for short-term earnings
- Unethical competitive practices
- Resentment from local communities that feel neglected and abandoned as companies go global and downsize
- Regulation and attacks by groups that mistrust corporate motives and agendas

And the list goes on and on, according to specific industry conditions.

When I ask the next question—what strategies have their organizations adopted to cope with these pressures?—an equally daunting list emerges, including the following:

- Intense scrutiny of costs and cost cutting to increase profits
- A tendency to downsize the workforce as a tactic to control labor costs and increase earnings

- Quality and service initiatives to meet customer demands
- Outsourcing of work to vendors and other countries with lower labor costs
- Technology investment to automate as many processes as possible
- Branding initiatives and other marketing initiatives to help create customer loyalty
- Increasing demands for more work for less money and greater employee productivity
- Constant reorganization and leadership churning
- Demand for greater speed to market to beat the competition, with a leadership mantra of "better, faster, and cheaper"

And then the coup de grace: how is all of this affecting employees and your ability to communicate with them about these subjects? How are your employees reacting? This is where it gets interesting, as they describe their workforce in the following terms:

- Cynical and distrustful of leadership motives
- Deeply insecure about their job tenure
- Willing to leave the company for the same or less money somewhere else
- Constantly pressured and stressed as the demands increase on their time and energy
- Burned out, exhausted by ever-increasing demands
- Angry
- Overloaded with information they can't process in the midst of pressured days
- Uninformed about strategy and changes that affect them, although simultaneously complaining that they're drowning in information overload

- Feeling entitled—and frustrated that no one recognizes their efforts
- Torn between family responsibilities and workplace demands

And then, finally, some brave soul inevitably, quietly, and somewhat reluctantly adds this:

- *But* excited about the challenges of change
- Motivated to help the company succeed
- Glad to have a job with a dynamic and changing organization
- Dedicated to do a job regardless of the adversity they face
- Anxious to contribute if they only understood management's expectations and future plans

And so it goes.

As I point out that this last set of mixed characteristics really describes the employee audience they are trying to reach and educate to today's challenges, I often see some squirming. Take a look, I say, at the lists. If your job is difficult, here's why. The communication professionals soberly nod and complain that they could help with all of this if only . . . If only their leadership would listen to their suggestions and recommendations. If only they were permitted to admit what everyone already knows anyway, as a means of preserving everyone's sanity. If only they had direct access to their leadership to help them cope with all of the above. Lots of "if only's."

The groups composed of corporate leaders generally also squirm. In one session, a Midwestern CEO asked me with some irritation, "What do you do if the receiver is broken? How do you get through in those cases?" That question of how you "get through" and get employees to see things "as we see them" is the common leadership lament.

An occasional reaction is dismissal. As one senior leader once exclaimed to me—when I observed that his employees must be upset about all the change they had experienced recently, including plant closings, relocation of company headquarters from Cleveland to Texas, and major downsizings—"Screw 'em." Not a typical reaction, but characteristic of the tough-guy approach to leadership.

The major culprit in what I am reporting is change with a capital C. The marketplace changed. The workforce itself certainly changed. The technology changed and gave people access to information they never had before, as well as a way to express their frustration. Leaders changed, as they were put under almost unbearable short-term financial pressures from large and small shareholders and security analysts. Most of all, the customers changed and demanded more for less as well as exercising their choices to go elsewhere if they didn't get exactly what they wanted and paid for, precisely when they wanted it. "Here it is; take it or leave it" is now, happily, a vestige of a bygone era. The difference clearly was that they now had choices and could in that sense hold their suppliers accountable for quality, price, and delivery.

Shifting Priorities and Constituencies

Historically, company leaders have argued that they had four major constituencies—customers, shareholders, employees, and the communities that housed their operations. With the coming of globalization and the intense competition it brought both internationally and locally, this foursome and its importance to the leadership shifted. Customers became more fickle and perfectly willing to go with the lowest-priced products and services rather than the brands to which they were traditionally loyal.

Shareholders and market analysts became more and more demanding of short-term results—a demand that was hardly lost on the senior leaders, whose bonuses and personal stock options depended on quarterly performance. The large pension funds, in their effort to find the best return on their fund's investment, held a club over the leaders that they were perfectly willing to use.

As it became increasingly profitable to move operations to low-wage countries, local communities had less and less power to hold onto the companies they depended on for employment and taxes. Dispersed operations became the strategy of choice for harassed CEOs, and those low wages looked more and more attractive as a way of cutting costs and overhead.

In this equation employees found themselves more and more expendable. The strategy of choice to increase the bottom line was to cut labor costs at unprecedented rates. For example, when I moved to Rochester in 1965, Kodak employed upwards of sixty thousand people in this community alone. With global competition and the rise of digital photography, Kodak found itself dependent on an increasingly obsolete technology that it had stubbornly sought to protect despite the handwriting on the wall. Today the Kodak workforce in Rochester numbers only some nine thousand and continues to decline.

When such layoff strategies were first employed, the companies that executed them were roundly criticized as cruel and unfeeling. But over time American society has become largely inured to such actions. Ten thousand here, fifteen thousand there—who cares, as long as they are not personally affected? Downsizing—that 1984ish euphemism that made the whole action seem so reasonable and neutral to those outside the organization—became respectable and even drew praise from the shareholder community looking for greater and greater return.

An Obvious Question

For me, in the midst of this chaotic change, the intriguing—and, I think, obvious—question all along has been: why don't we recognize and act on the simple truth that a company's work-force is the ultimate engine that makes the organization do what everyone wants? Or if we do recognize it, why don't we do something about it? Why don't we appreciate that regardless of all of the countervailing pressures, the company's employees (whether we call them "associates" or "colleagues" or just plain "workers") are the company's new primary capital asset? That fact was always given loud lip service, but lip service it mostly was, as employees continue to be listed only on the balance sheet as a cost of doing business, never as a company asset.

As *Harvard Business Review* editor Tom Stewart points out in his fascinating book *Intellectual Capital*, today's organization can have all of the money and resources in the world and not be competitive if it doesn't have the right workforce in place, creating the intellectual capital the organization needs for the sake of innovation and growth. And as authors like Robert Reich in *The Future of Success*, Thomas Friedman in *The World Is Flat,* and others have made clear, a company's talented people represent the one capital asset that can't be duplicated by the competition.

Companies can catch up technologically. They can compete on the basis of price. But neither of these is a lasting advantage. The only true lasting competitive advantage they have is a smart, dedicated, informed, and engaged workforce—particularly when, as now, we are in an economic and social revolution that is akin to the Industrial Revolution and the movement from agriculture to manufacturing. Except this time, it's from a manufacturing to a service to an information economy. Revolutionary change. No doubt about it.

In an information economy, the actual raw material is information itself. The modern assembly line in the Information Age is virtual, manned by smart, educated people who take that raw information, add their expertise to it, and pass it on to their peers, who in turn add or modify what they receive in producing the intellectual capital that is the basis of improved products and services. Intellectual capital is the real treasure of any organization today. And only well-informed and engaged people can create it.

To do so, they clearly need to be informed about goals, strategy, vision, mission, and a myriad of operating priorities and issues.

How Things Got This Way

After pondering for some time why so many companies today regard the workforce primarily as a cost that can be depreciated and eventually written off, I think I understand the complex set of causes that led to a devaluation of the workforce and their contributions.

One is the historical nature of work in what was mainly an industrial economy in this country for almost 150 years. The notion of "if you don't like it here, go somewhere else because there are twenty people in line who can replace you" is a vestige of that industrial economy. It's no longer true in an information economy. What happens if the lead heart surgeon leaves a hospital staff? What happens if the brightest engineers desert their Silicon Valley start-up? How about the talented sales person with a myriad of important personal contacts? Or the investment banker who understands the convoluted intricacies of mergers and acquisitions better than anyone else on staff? Or, for that matter, the manufacturing operator who runs a technically complex piece of machinery that needs special care and attention? None of those people is expendable or easily replaced, regardless of how large or small a talent pool is waiting outside the gates. And increasingly these are the workers who are more and more representative of today's workforce in the Information Age.

Another factor in the devaluing of a company's people is the competing priorities faced by senior leaders. Today such leaders are evaluated by one standard and one standard alone: Has the company performed according to expectations? Not "Has it *performed?*" but "Has it met the arbitrary estimates of Wall Street analysts who follow its fortunes (as well as expectations of the shareholders who bet on a quick return from that performance)?" These pressures are hard to resist, especially by CEOs with shorter and shorter tenure—and golden parachutes securely strapped on.

Still another factor is global competition. The onetime monopoly of American companies has been broken in industry after industry. In fact, much of our manufacturing capability and capacity has left our shores for lower-labor-cost economies in countries like China, India, and other developing countries. In those cases it's easy to dismiss the value of a higher-paid workforce and even to search for ways to lessen any dependence on them. American leaders under intense pressure to deliver bottom-line results often give in to the temptation to downsize their American workforce and to expand outside of the United States.

But I see growing and encouraging evidence of leadership's willingness to mend its ways and finally give credence to "people as our most valuable asset." One of the most encouraging developments is the employee engagement movement and its attempts to find ways to unleash the discretionary effort of the workforce. Another is the growing realization that customer satisfaction and service are much more likely to be products of an informed and motivated workforce.

So the purpose of this book is to encourage that willingness and to offer strategic advice as to what works and what doesn't work in today's chaotically changing world. Communication is the undoubted lubricant to prevent the corporate machinery from self-destructing from the friction of change.

Let's begin first with an example I call a morality tale, so we understand what *not* to do, as counterpoint before I offer a whole series of prescriptions for communication success. This first example I will cite is one I lived through and that for me is a classic and instructive case of how so many otherwise effective organizations bungle both change management and communication. For me, for some years now, it has been a metaphor for the plight of a company overwhelmed by change. As I say, it's a tale with a moral.

The Credible Company

.

1

A MORALITY TALE

In the summer of 1981 Xerox Corporation was poised on the edge of a cliff. Few people, except the most senior leadership, understood just how precarious the company's position was.

Ironically, that same summer a proposed "full employment" policy had been circulating for approval. According to its terms, Xerox would emulate what were then policies of its competitor IBM and essentially promise that no one who had reached a certain level of competence and service could be fired. They might be "redeployed" to another position, but they would essentially have lifetime job security.

When I read the policy draft as the manager of employee communication for Xerox's copier division based in Rochester, New York, I was delighted that I was part of a company that was determined to continue its long-standing progressive employment policies. This would be the culmination of years of corporate enlightenment by one of the country's true glamour companies. It's hard to appreciate it today, but Xerox during the 1960s and '70s was the Microsoft of that era; it held a virtual monopoly on the copier business until global competition and patent and antitrust lawsuits from prospective competitors finally broke its hold.

So the shock was even more intense when, in early fall, my boss called me into his office and told me in confidence that Xerox leadership was concocting a plan to lay off up to 15 percent of its global workforce. I was stunned. How could this have happened so fast? We had been talking about full employment a few weeks before, and now the leadership was reversing itself entirely and quietly using the new term *downsizing* in secret meetings to describe its plan for the near-term future.

What the hell did downsizing mean, anyway? Clearly it was a euphemism for a devastating policy reversal. As a responsible communication professional, how was I to incorporate such a 1984-ish word into our vocabulary? And when was all of this going to happen? And, more to the point, *why* was it happening? I peppered my boss with questions that he clearly had no specific answers to. All he could say was that business results were down severely. Later I was to discover just how severely.

When I first joined Xerox in 1968, we had a 97-percent share of the plain paper copying market. I knew that competition had been eating at our market share in the last several years, but I had no idea how severe the erosion was. The truth that had not been shared outside of senior leadership circles was that our market share had dropped so precipitously over the last three years that at that point it was below 15 percent. It's beyond the scope of this tale—and this book—to detail all the reasons, but we were clearly a company in deep trouble.

Once I recovered from the shock of the proposed downsizing action, I immediately reacted with a suggestion that we had better begin to design a communication strategy to explain this devastating turn of events. I said "devastating" because downsizing in 1981 was far from the commonplace corporate strategy it has become over the last quarter of a century. Clearly, we had to tell our people not only what was happening but why it was happening. And the story had better be good—in short, truthful, candid, and timely—so people could absorb the inevitable shock. Few Xerox people had a clue that their comfortable world was about to be rocked.

Xerox, under the enthusiastic leadership of CEO Dave Kearns, had long had a reputation for an enlightened internal communication process, with open sharing of both good and bad news. As at all companies, the balance was predominantly on the positive side with a smattering of the negative to keep things honest. But

I was honestly taken aback after I presented what I thought was a well-conceived and sensitive communication strategy to my boss a few days later. His response, once he had circulated it to our leadership, was, "They're not buying it. They don't want to talk."

Surely I couldn't be hearing him right. How could we not "talk" about an action that was bound to bring the media pounding at our door to find out the real story of our problems? Not to mention how our own employees were going to react. How could we possibly think that we could somehow carry out this action under the cover of darkness or public indifference? The Wall Street analysts would be all over us, as well as our shareholders. Not talk? That was a recipe for disaster.

He agreed, but asked me to revise the communication strategy I had prepared for our employees so that it was not quite so threatening to the psyche of our leaders. Reluctantly, I complied and toned down some of the messages to make them a little less threatening while still conveying the difficult circumstances we faced.

He called corporate headquarters in Stamford, Connecticut, where he and his human resource counterparts tried to prevail on Dave Kearns and his senior staff to consider a more forthcoming strategy—particularly with our employees. I lobbied with my corporate communication counterpart to do the same. The reply was the same as before: "We're not interested. We don't want to talk about this. We're just going to do it and let the fact speak for itself." I was both disheartened and concerned for what I knew would be the inevitable consequences as our people struggled to figure out what was happening and what it meant to their respective situations.

If this is all beginning to sound a bit overwrought, consider that Xerox was a company that ever since the introduction of the 914 copier (heralded as the most successful new product in history) had experienced unprecedented growth and profit with few warning signs of misfortune—at least few that anyone wanted to believe. In fact, this was "the company that could"; the one under whose technical leadership the development of plain paper copying had been achieved when everyone else—including IBM, 3M, and Kodak—had rejected the idea as unfeasible. In retrospect, it was a setup for the arrogance that almost always overcomes common sense in companies in such circumstances. The inevitable fall is hard to conceive, let alone accept.

Not long after the initial planning for the downsizing, Kearns made what turned out to be an ill-advised visit to Rochester to speak with a group of Xerox managers and professionals. He quietly broke the news to what he thought was an insider group who would keep it to themselves. Predictably, the local papers picked up the story and reported it from "an unidentified source." When asked, Xerox media people would not confirm or deny any of it, undoubtedly believing that Kearns had been burned by people he trusted with confidential information.

The ensuing weeks were a nightmare, as Xerox maintained its silence while local reporters and other media bombarded the company and its employees with questions. The employee rumor mill went wild with all sorts of speculation that inevitably inflated the 15-percent number. Fear and insecurity fueled a serious drop in employee morale as people began considering their futures and the possibility they would be part of the 15 percent or whatever number they had heard. The best performers, as they always do in such situations, began to contemplate their multiple job options.

It got so bad at one point that the local paper reported a joke that had been circulating in the company and was supplied by an employee who had called to urge them to get "the real story." The joke: what's the difference between Xerox and the *Titanic*? The answer: the *Titanic* had a band. Gallows humor personified.

When the by-then widely expected layoffs began in Rochester, where the bulk of company employees were located, the first media call to Xerox public relations that day was from the *London Times*. The next two were from the *Wall Street Journal* and the *New York Times*. And so it went. The poor media spokesperson was reduced to a "No comment" reply. So much for keeping the action quiet, as banner stories ran in all of the media the next day.

All of that ushered in more than a year and a few months of a kind of Chinese water torture for the workforce, as layoffs continued throughout major pockets of the company. Finally Kearns and his senior leaders launched a full-scale strategy review leading to an eventual initiative dubbed "Leadership Through Quality." Kearns later admitted, in a candid book entitled *Prophets in the Dark* (coauthored with his trusted outside consultant David Nadler), that he feared his collapsing company would wind up being sold in a fire sale if he and his senior staff didn't do something drastic.

Alarmed and rattled by the rapid decline of market share, he initiated a series of actions to stop the bleeding and implemented policies that helped the company slowly recover. By 1989 the effort was so successful that Xerox won the coveted Baldridge Award for its manufacturing quality. Lack of uniform product quality and reliability had been at least partially to blame for the stunning market share and revenue reversals. So the Baldridge Award marked a critical turning point after some seven years of tough sledding. The damage, however, had been done. It took several years for Xerox to recover the respect and employee trust that had marked its earlier history of enlightened leadership. (Much later, in the 1990s, miscues by a new generation of Xerox leaders once again threatened the company's reputation and welfare through a series of accounting misadventures and strategic errors. It seems all too often that corporate memories are painfully short. But that's another story.)

A Tale Worth Considering

Why do I bother beginning a book on employee communication by retelling this painful story some decades later, especially when such actions no longer shock us as they once did? And when most of the principals have long since left the scene? The answer is that in my mind it is a morality tale from which we can learn much. Additionally, it was an important bit of foreshadowing of the events that have created a skeptical, mistrusting workforce in many, if not most, of our large corporate organizations today.

If indeed the past is prologue, what lessons can we derive from the Xerox debacle? One of the perhaps more obvious ones is the need for senior leaders and communication professionals to work together in such situations. My problem all those years ago, frankly, was that I was too low on the food chain. I had to present my case only through intermediaries, who may or may not have had the understanding or background to press the point as aggressively as I wished. All I could do was accept the verdicts they brought back to me and push back as hard as my position permitted. In the interest of full disclosure here, I was so distressed by the unfolding of this scenario that I resigned. My logic was that if I could not affect a situation as dramatic as this, there was no sense in staying on. So I quit after a thirteen-year career at Xerox during which I had watched the company experience explosive growth and eventually face its roller-coaster ride to near disaster.

In any effective communication strategy it is imperative that the senior leaders and the communication professionals work closely together to craft and execute the strategy. They are the two key parties in a time of troubles, one to lead confidently and the other to help explain. For this reason this book is addressed to both leaders and communication professionals in the hopes that it will help influence greater mutual cooperation in the face of communication challenges.

In the Xerox case the internal communication team should have joined hands with their external counterparts in pressing the senior staff to do the right thing and communicate as openly as the situation permitted. No one would have advocated a path that could damage the company, but together with David Kearns and his staff we could have minimized the eventual damage that was done to employee morale and to the faith of the company's major constituencies. Instead, we were relegated to the role of bystanders who had to explain the company's dire situation and the actions to be taken after the fact. By then the damage had been done, and any possibility of getting proactively out ahead of this story was lost.

The last straw for me was a visit to corporate headquarters the week the rolling layoffs began. I was dismayed to see an advance copy of *Xerox World*, the newspaper that was distributed to all employees that week—without a single mention of the actions already under way and widely known about among employees. I recall turning to my colleagues with a mixture of frustration and anger and asking them if I was the only one who was struck by this glaring and insulting omission. I was met with mixed expressions of guilt and embarrassment. It was surreal, as if none of this problem or process was worth reporting. The silence had been carried to the point of pretense and denial. That was the day I decided to resign.

The other—and more important—lesson was what happened to employees and their trust of their own leadership. Sadly, this lesson seems to be repeated over and over again without people learning how to avoid it. I have no way of measuring the morale impact, but I know for a fact that employee productivity crashed in the first few weeks when the story was leaking out like a gush of water from a ruptured water line. People were totally distracted as they gathered in small, worried groups to try to determine what it all meant to them personally.

In the short term there is no question that downsizing layoffs can relieve the financial or other pressures that a company is under. But the long-term costs can be devastating. For example, before the Xerox cutbacks the company in 1981 achieved operating profits of nearly $1.15 billion, which was the best performance in company history. In 1982 earnings crashed to half that number: $614 million. The impact on employees and shareholders alike was devastating as customers deserted Xerox products for those of the competition. In this case the "long-term" results of the debacle came along faster than anyone could have imagined.

One of the great ironies of change communication is that it seldom answers the most important question on the minds of each and every employee—namely, what's going to happen to me? Employees typically are in a very vulnerable condition when it comes to their employment security. They have obligations and dependents to worry about, and the understanding of their vulnerability in a downsizing leads to an all-pervasive, free-floating anxiety that affects every aspect of their work.

The usual response of company leaders is, we don't have answers so we will decline to engage those individual questions. That strikes them as a reasonable response, but it's not. In my experience, short of mergers, plant closings, sell-offs of whole divisions, and the like, we have a pretty good idea of who is or is not expendable. If that's true, why can't individual managers identify employees at risk in a downsizing and communicate their vulnerability to them so that they can begin to plan their futures as well as their circumstances permit? Equipped with that knowledge, they can better cope with a very threatening personal situation.

In the Xerox case the leadership chose to follow the most painful path of all: keeping employees in a constant state of anxiety over an extended period of time. Unfortunately, too many senior leaders follow this same nonstrategy based on the argument that they simply don't know how events are going to unfold. Fair enough. Then at least give people a sense of their potential risk. The counterargument is that employee productivity and morale will decline. Who's kidding whom? It's already in the toilet because of the prevailing uncertainty.

The other issue here is the need to restore faith in the leadership's ability to lead. There is a predicable chain of employee reaction in the face of negative change. The first reaction, once people understand the threat, is, How did this happen? What events led to our present dilemma?

The second and predictably human reaction is, Who's to blame? Let's identify him or her and inflict a proper punishment. Consider any case in which people decide that harm is done to them because of leadership incompetence. Think even of natural events like hurricanes or other disastrous phenomena. One of the inevitable stages when people's patience runs short is to call for the heads of those they deem responsible for not either warning them or taking the proper remedial action. This phenomenon also explains why there are so many government probes, hearings, and special investigations. We have a powerful need to fix blame and seek revenge.

If people manage to get past this feeling, they move to a more positive position. Their next question is, what is your future plan to prevent recurrences? In the Xerox case and in every similar case I've seen as a consultant, people go through these predictable changes. At Xerox the cry was, What's our strategy to get out of this mess? What's the battle plan?

It's not hard to understand why people respond like this. They want a sense that the leadership understands the present causes, is searching actively for remedies, and has a concrete plan to move forward. In fact, the simplest formula for effective employee communication in any organization is to answer three questions: Where are we going? How do we propose to get there? And what does all of that mean to me?

So the lessons are clear. Senior leaders and communication professionals need to be honest with one another and in partnership to communicate simply, clearly, and in a timely fashion about the trends, events, and needs that knit the people in an organization together. They also need a clear understanding of the human psyche and human needs on the job as well as how people respond to change. Armed with those understandings and the all-important will to do the right thing, they can communicate even the most painful of events and intentions.

Who Does It Right?

The Xerox case I've described here—which is replicated regularly by more organizations than I can count—is a case of what not to do. As a consultant, I am constantly asked to name companies that "do it right" and communicate effectively with their employees and other constituencies. It's a question I dislike intensely because, frankly, I see so few examples of doing it right. And the ones I do see are usually fragmentary successes. To some extent, this has been my experience because consultants, like doctors, spend most of their time seeing sick patients or those with nasty symptoms rather than healthy ones. But much of it has to do with leadership unwillingness to admit problems or flaws and to opt instead for spin or for silence.

My reluctance to answer, however, actually begs the question. Is there a logical and successful strategy to inform skeptical employees in a time of turbulent change? After spending more than four decades as a corporate communication executive and consultant, I have discovered that there indeed is a set of principles or insights that, if employed properly, constitute a kind of formula for success.

I tend to distrust handy dandy formulas or the often desired silver bullet that my clients sometimes seek. But I know from experience that there are some seven principles that make a vital difference if they are properly understood and employed. All of these are interrelated and need to be part of a continuing and well-considered communication strategy regardless of a company's fortunes at any point in time. They are particularly important in providing a skeptical workforce with the insights and information they need to perform effectively.

The rest of this book will define and explain those seven principles as a prescription for any organization that hopes to communicate in a way that creates employee enthusiasm and commitment as well as trust. Here's a brief look at the principles I'll flesh out in the coming chapters:

Principle One: Information

The obvious first requirement of solid communication is reliable, accurate, and timely information. Today, when so much of the value that organizations represent is found in their intellectual capital, information is truly the raw material for a kind of intellectual capital assembly line. If you think about it, much of the work in contemporary organizations has to do with passing information from one group to another and adding to it the particular experience and wisdom of the team members. Done properly, what emerges from this assembly line is knowledge that can be used to create new products and services that constitute the organization's precious intellectual capital.

Principle Two: Needs of the Audience

By *needs* I refer to the human needs that every worker, regardless of his or her position in the organization, brings to work. What kind of communication do we require to stay focused and to want to give our best to the organization of which we are a part? What sorts of communication are likely to make us more engaged in our work? Conversely, what kinds of communication tend to turn us off and to create mistrust and alienation? These are vital questions for any organization that hopes to be competitive in a dog-eat-dog global environment.

Principle Three: Face-to-Face Communication

The employee research has made the same point for years and years. Given a choice, people prefer to receive important information about their jobs face-to-face with another human being. That person generally is their immediate manager or supervisor. Why this is so is not really hard to understand. We are social animals who depend on visual and verbal clues to understand our reality. Evolution has determined this bias as a mechanism to trigger our fight-or-flight response, that inborn self-protection that governs whether we feel endangered or not and what we will do about it.

It's not surprising that this behavior carries over into organizations whose environments can often seem to be threatening to the individual as a result of competition, personal insecurity, and the high stakes that generally typify life in a highly structured organization.

Principle Four: Openness

The notion of organizational openness is another important communication issue. Closed organizations inevitably arouse distrust and suspicion. The human reaction is that somehow secretiveness and the necessity to hide something unpleasant go hand in hand. Yet there are perfectly valid reasons for organizations to protect their best interests by keeping some secrets.

The guiding principle for sharing information with company employees should be that all information in the organization—except for proprietary, competitive, and personal information—is fair game. In general, the more open an organization is, particularly to the people responsible for doing the work, the more successful it will be in its marketplace.

Principle Five: Research

All organizations are similar in their structures and missions, but they all are also different from one another. Understanding those differences in your own organization is a must. What is the collective vision of your leadership for the organization they lead together? What is their specific agenda in achieving that vision and its accompanying mission? What are their most important business priorities? What values do they truly hold and, more important, live by, in carrying out their leadership responsibilities?

What about the employees who make up your organization's workforce? How well do they understand the direction and priorities of their organization? Do they have what we commonly refer to as a "line of sight" between what they do and what the organization is trying to achieve? Do they understand the marketplace in which their organization is operating and the connection between the marketplace and the company strategy that is a response to that marketplace? Do they understand and accept the brand promise? More to the point, are they willing to make that promise real through their behavior and attitudes?

Gathering this all important data is the first step in a kind of market research of employee needs.

Principle Six: Marketplace and Workplace

The trouble with organizations facing serious change (and that includes just about all of them today) is that people tend to lose their focus in the midst of the chaos and urgency the organization faces. The temptation at such times is to turn inward and focus on internal problems and their solution. What is needed instead is a focus on the external marketplace and how it is driving strategy. Change severs our comfortable connections, so we need to make connections to the new realities.

Another problem with change is that it usually is chaotic and unpredictable as well as never ending. To survive, we need to have a frame of reference to show us where Corporate North is on our internal compass. The marketplace gives us a sense of *why* we need a new coping strategy. When that new strategy is explained in terms of the market forces that justify and legitimize it, a newfound credibility and understanding informs all sorts of otherwise random and chaotic events.

Principle Seven: Strategy

Most of us, when confronted with a problem, tend to immediately begin thinking of potential solutions. So it's only natural that this tendency also affects the leadership of an organization when confronted with the need to inform the workforce of an important development. The first inclination is to concoct the right message to convey the development. The second is to search for the best channel or channels to deliver the message. And much of this occurs under serious time pressures presenting a sense of urgency that overcomes intelligent communication strategy. It is reactive communication personified.

The more intelligent approach is a proactive communication strategy based on audience needs and focused mainly on communicating the issues of the organization as a framework for understanding. When that is done well, the news event, whatever it is, can be explained in terms of the organization's priorities and issues. In that case it is far less disruptive than if it is simply delivered as a piece of raw news without further context. The lack of context is what tends to create unnecessary speculation and consternation in organizations.

Combining Principles into a Coherent Whole

The obvious test of good communication is its ability to truly inform the reader or listener. In fact, the question "Who does it right?" that I dislike so much—which triggered this list of principles—can be answered only by reference to these same principles. If you're like me and have trouble organizing and remembering a bunch of seemingly unrelated principles, let me offer you a device that organizes this book's overall message. Look at the first letters of each of the seven principles. Their initial letters— Information, Needs of the audience, Face-to-face communication, Openness, Research, Marketplace, and Strategy—form the acronym INFORMS.

Why resort to such a contrived device to keep this all straight? Acronyms are simple and memorable, and I want to communicate to you a memorable prescription for effective communication to and with a skeptical audience, for that is the basic attitude and posture of today's workforce. We want and need communication that *informs* that workforce and that helps them understand and commit to intelligent strategies and ethical leaderships. To carry on that kind of informing, we need to deliberately and proactively manage the communication process.

And that's the essential point. Communication is a process, not a series of activities, campaigns, or projects. Nor is it,
as some suggest, merely "internal journalism." It's not a series of
news bulletins or, even worse, a collection of tactics, tools, and
channels. For the employee it is like the air he or she breathes at
work. Ask any group of employees what the word *communication*
means to them, and you will soon be into an extended conversation of everything from the degree of trust they have in their
leadership to the need to keep the company directory up to date
or their machines calibrated so that they can produce the kind
of quality their leaders demand.

It's not the imprecision of the word so much as it is the fact
that communication is the robust process that keeps us joined
together in common enterprises. It informs our actions and
permits us to see the relevance of our lives in a chaotic world.
(How's that for a high-falutin', but deadly accurate, definition?)

In the following chapters I'll explain the seven principles
in my prescription and provide examples and stories of what
I mean by each one. Taken together and carefully executed,
these principles will at last permit you to inform an otherwise
skeptical and jaded employee audience.

2

INFORMATION

There's obviously no way to cover a subject as enormous as *information* in a chapter, so I'll confine my remarks here to the relationship between information as raw material and the responsibilities of any corporate communication person in helping deliver and manage it. That relationship is more complex than ever before as a result of explosively developing technology that challenges and excites the imagination of communication professionals in unprecedented ways.

What should be their new responsibilities in the face of that challenge? What opportunities does technology present for them to change their roles within the organization and help it perform more effectively? How does technology affect a proper conception of that role and its urgencies? What information is essential and valuable? What is a waste of both time and limited audience attention and energy? These are all pertinent and difficult questions in a rapidly changing corporate environment, and it will take a fair amount of trial, error, and experimentation in each organization to provide solid answers.

Historically, company communication professionals have tended to see their role as information purveyors—shaping it, getting it approved for distribution, delivering it through tried and tested channels, listening to audience reactions, correcting misimpressions and inaccuracies, and, in the best case, acting as information advisors. The trouble with being a purveyor is the risk of losing objectivity about the good or ill effects of information and even believing that all information is equal in importance and value.

Purveyors tend to be media- and project-focused rather than process-focused. The distinction is an important one. Projects have a beginning, middle, and end. Process is ongoing and requires continuing attention. I have long believed that there are two kinds of communication professionals—those who are project people, who see their work in terms of discrete tasks with finite timelines, and those who are comfortable with the ambiguity of process. The project people tend to see communication as a series of tasks to be addressed one by one; after each is completed, they move on to the next discrete project. In contrast, the process people see communication as an all-encompassing and never-ending challenge that requires a careful strategy to address the needs of the audience. In this case I'm firmly on the side of the process people.

To say we are living in an information society is to restate a well-worn cliché. Information is the lifeblood of the modern corporate world. Without accurate and timely information in this emerging technological society, we are lost. Yet information is only the raw material for understanding. Understanding is our ultimate need, so we must be very careful about how we view and process information.

The technology revolution has infinitely complicated this question. We now have the power to process and transmit information at unprecedented rates of speed. But that same speed can distort information by delivering it before it has been properly vetted for its accuracy, truthfulness, and value. All too often speed is the enemy of understanding—and certainly of reflection.

In today's time-pressured workplace, in which technology has imposed this new urgency for speed, we must be very careful to value reflection and to seek understanding as well as speedy message delivery. Instant communication may well be just too fast to enable human understanding. Yes, information is a critical raw material in today's society. But it is also subject to distortion and stupefying overproduction.

Having said that, it's easy to understate just how extensively the *need* for accurate and useable information has expanded. That need is largely fed by the fact that information today is the raw material for a contemporary assembly line. The old assembly line, perfected by Henry Ford and his industrial engineers, required people to assemble products in an efficient line where they took parts from nearby bins, complex overhead mechanisms, or moving belts and put them together according to an unwavering plan. Speed and efficiency were paramount.

It was in the manufacturing environment of the late 1800s and the early 1900s that efficiency expert Frederick Winslow Taylor offered his famous dictum that all the worker needed to know was who his boss was and what he wanted him to do right now. Mindlessness was the order of the day for that worker, valued only for his strength and ability to follow orders within a rigid system designed to limit personal innovation or choices.

The New Assembly Line

In contrast, the twenty-first-century company's assembly line is more likely to be an intellectual system enabled by technology. That system allows people to share information as raw material to be shaped and improved and then passed on to coworkers for their contribution. The chief objective is to create intellectual capital from human knowledge and experience. The production of that intellectual capital, which is the only real basis for innovation and improved products and services, is the contemporary equivalent of spinning straw into gold. Except in this case, the straw is information and the spinning wheel is this virtual assembly line.

In a highly competitive economy with infinite customer choice of products and services, intellectual capital is the most precious asset a company can have. It is now as vital as investor capital, if not more so. Today you can have all of the investor capital in the world to purchase the buildings, parts, and machinery that made the old industrial economy go, but if you don't have the necessary human capital—the informed and knowledgeable people who make up the new assembly line—you have nothing. And without useable information, today's intellectual capital assembly line grinds to a halt.

Information Requirements and a New Opportunity

What does all of this have to do with the role of the communication professional in today's organization? If he or she is truly a communication expert, there is a new and important opportunity not only to influence the communication *outputs* of the organization but also to have an impact on *outcomes*— an impact, in fact, on the very performance of the information assembly line and ultimately the performance of the company.

Consider the qualities of the information required by the contemporary knowledge worker. First is timeliness. In an economy with *better, faster, cheaper* as its competitive mantra, it does no good, for example, for the sales force to get the latest information on the new product two or three weeks or months after the product promotion is under way. During that time lag, they are repeatedly at a loss to capitalize on the promotion as customers confront them with new product questions for which they have no answers. Such time lags become a clear barrier to performance.

Nor, obviously, does it do the user any good to receive inaccurate information. Too often, in a stressful environment characterized by demands for speed, unprocessed information is rushed to work stations before it has been vetted to be certain that it represents the latest and most complete and accurate data. Incorrect plans in a manufacturing environment, customer requirements poorly communicated to engineers during a design cycle, misunderstood customer priorities hastily communicated to a team writing an important sales proposal—all these and more result in not only the ultimate user's wasting precious time and productivity but also lost opportunity and production.

Another problem is incomplete information. Leaving out that one key piece of the puzzle can easily cripple the intellectual capital building process. Neglect or ignorance of the process, disengagement, a lack of interest in the success of the process, and simply not recognizing that others may need that one missing piece to complete the solution all contribute to the delivery of incomplete information.

Finally, there is the serious obstacle of mixed messages from the leadership. For example, "We want quality, but be careful not to expend too much money or time on this process or activity." Given a choice, most assembly-line members will read that to mean that quality is secondary to the cost of producing the product or service. Leaders need to be extremely careful about delivering mixed messages that can subvert the very process that is critical to the company's success.

In a professional services environment, for example, it is tempting to communicate an order for the avoidance of any activity or research that is not directly billable to a client. The demand for billable hours in those environments is intense and urgent. But giving in to that temptation can easily lead to a lack of company creativity or innovation and finally to stagnation in the company's services. Taken to extremes, it can even affect the company's ability to compete in a rapidly changing competitive environment with new client demands.

Another familiar example is the company call center, where too often the communicated task is to dispatch the customer as quickly as possible rather than to deal with his or her concern. The order from the top is to not spend too much time on any one call. The driving force and the supposed efficiency measure is the number of calls handled by someone who is allegedly a customer service representative, rather than the quality of service provided to the customer.

In several companies I've worked with, I've seen this phenomenon at work. What usually suffers most is the real objective of the leadership. It is rare that employees are sufficiently informed about leadership motive, priorities, and intention to deal with subtle choices, so they will err on the side of caution, past history, or personal frustration. Too often the result is a jaded worker who feels that her leadership, working at fifty thousand feet, simply doesn't understand the issues at her level. Or she sees the cautions as contradictory to why she was hired in the first place and therefore perceives any leadership comments about the importance of customer service as lip service or a lie. The mixed message clearly degrades any serious attempt at providing service.

Information and Business Performance: From Outputs to Outcomes

Some of the issues we're discussing may strike you initially as beyond the interest or control of the traditional communication professional. That's especially true if you see that person as only an information purveyor as opposed to a communication problem solver. But the issue is vital to performance in a networked organization, in which information must flow horizontally across silo and turf boundaries to meet the needs of the intellectual capital assembly line.

It also represents an important new opportunity for those who are the organization's supposed communication experts. Given that the typical worker sees communication and information as being more like the very air he or she breathes than as a set of formalized channels that deliver carefully scrubbed leadership messages, a new mindset about the potential role of communication in organizations may well be in order.

That mindset has been championed by consultant and author Jim Shaffer, among others. He complains that the input-based function (that is, one that focuses only on leadership information delivery through traditional communication media) has been preoccupied with the formal communication channels and their effectiveness, at the expense of the broader communication process. He asserts that without sufficient attention to improving the information-delivery system to better serve the needs of customers and the priorities of the organization, communication professionals are not adding much measurable value to business results.

Multiple forces are combining to require a change in that traditional media and channel focus. Business leaders increasingly insist that the communication function, like other business functions, add measurable value. So communication management needs to focus on the outcomes of communication, to determine how to minimize or eliminate the ubiquitous communication breakdowns that cause people and their organizations to underperform.

Internal communication professionals need to reconsider their roles and not be afraid to get down and dirty in the communication trenches, to tackle the operating problems that represent the real communication concerns of both their leadership and their employee audience. That means first finding out from the leadership their most important business priorities and then determining if there are information breakdowns or misunderstandings that undermine those priorities and cause poor performance.

Practically any work team can readily identify the day-to-day communication failures and obstacles that frustrate their best efforts. Unfortunately, too often they resign themselves over time to the view that such failures are an inherent feature of organizational life or leader indifference that they must live with as best they can. The task then is to work with such natural work teams to determine just where and how the information assembly line is malfunctioning or breaking down and undermining performance.

Once that's understood, it is a relatively simple matter to begin finding the actual causes of communication misfires and determining solutions that will improve the effectiveness of a process. Shaffer, by working with a variety of clients in a process that is truly communication detective work in seeking the root causes of communication failures and breakdowns, has achieved remarkable improvements in the transmission and efficiency of the raw information so critical to efficiency and performance. Those improvements, in turn, lead to important cost savings that flow directly to the bottom line.

One simple example may serve to make the point. FedEx Express, the original core business of FedEx, did a global communication assessment that revealed huge opportunities to address one of the company's primary strategic objectives—namely, to increase the number of packages they exported from the United States.

Drawing on various internal disciplines and convening a knowledgeable Los Angeles–based team of fifteen people who could most influence export volume, Shaffer and the team carefully analyzed what was not working, and why, in the overall communication process. They looked at all of the team relationships as well as the incentives that were influencing or incenting the performance of the various individuals who were critical to process success.

Based on their final recommendations, the company piloted an intense communication initiative to increase both customer and employee understanding of the needs and workings of FedEx Express's export business. The final result of their work was to improve sales and operations integration and shift the emphasis of a courier incentive plan from one that implied that domestic business was more important than export business to one that balanced the importance of the two lines of business equally.

In the first four months of the pilot effort, export volume increased by 15 percent and sales went up 23 percent. Overall, the project created a nearly 1500-percent return on the cost of its investment in the team's effort. The company replicated the effort in five more locations and generated an impressive additional 1660-percent ROI.

This pioneering work obviously moves communication professionals to a very different operational role from the traditional one they've played. It shifts their emphasis from communication programs and channels to matching communication process to operational performance. The goal is to make work processes more responsive to business objectives and customer needs—an obvious priority of all business leaders.

The Challenge

Clearly, that movement from simply delivering information to a mass employee audience to getting into the grit of actual work processes takes the communication professional to the heart of what communication does or does not do to advance the business objectives of an organization. Because so many of us who have served in traditional communication roles come from non-operational backgrounds like public relations or journalism, this transition is not only bit of culture shock but also a significant professional challenge. Indeed, many people can't actually make the journey because of their lack of business sophistication or their discomfort with communication as a robust operating process rather than a simple means of message delivery. They also worry, with some justification, whether their leadership and the rest of the organization will accept them in this changed role, so a lot of discussion and adjusting has to take place on all sides of that issue.

Some critics of this approach argue that it makes the communication process too focused on measurable customer and process efficiencies at the expense of the larger mission of informing and motivating the workforce to create greater levels of engagement in the work. They claim that this "hearts and minds" mission should be the real focus of organizational communication.

The interesting question is, can people be taught to be both—the purveyor of inspiration and education, on the one hand, and the communication detective and problem solver, on the other? Although it's admittedly not a simple transition, I think in many instances, with training and immersion in the operating problems of the business, it can be done. It's a matter of becoming a problem solver and thoughtful observer as well as an educator and thinker who understands how to reach a diverse audience. It also takes a solid understanding of the needs and priorities of the business, along with a rapport with the people who do the difficult day-to-day operational work of an organization. And of course it also takes the confidence to surface problems and conceive and propose solutions. It's obviously not everyone's cup of tea, but for the communication professional willing to adapt to its challenges, it's a possible new and significant value-added role in information management and delivery.

Technology and Its Information Consequences

There is no question that the flow of information in organizations has become a flood, thanks to the technology explosion we've experienced in recent years. As one acquaintance recently stated, "If I had said to anyone in the year 2000 that the company telephone would be largely put on hold and that we would become essentially a letter-writing society, they would have written me off as a nut. And yet with email, that's exactly what's happened. Try to get a live person on a phone these days. You're better off writing them an email and starting an endless chain of send and reply."

That's but one small example of what communication technology has wrought in the process of moving information quickly from one person to another. The ubiquitous cell phone and the BlackBerry and its ilk—practically a cell phone on steroids— have completed the scenario of a society of citizens electronically joined at the ear.

Computer technology in the workplace is a double-edged sword. Living with it has created a whole series of new issues.

Living without it has become unthinkable. The enabling power of technology is amazing by virtue of its versatile applications, speed of transmission, graphics quality, accessibility to data, and previously unheard-of computing power. As the means of collaboration and information sharing, it can enable organizations to obtain a competitive edge, reduce product and manufacturing cycles, and speed products and services to market. It can also help create the image of a company that is more far-sighted and innovative than its competitors, that truly is on the leading edge both as a producer and as an attractive employer for the savvy computer generation that has grown up with it as an essential accompaniment of their lives and activities.

But there is an undoubted downside. I make that point with some trepidation. Because we are presently in a love affair with our various technological gadgets, any expression of reservations is likely to lead to misunderstanding. If I have a quarrel with the technologists, it is not with their technology. That would be a ridiculous position. Rather, it's with those who see it as an end in itself rather than a means or who are unwilling to admit any downside. Also, the last impression I want to leave is that I am somehow a neo-Luddite.

But because we are in the infancy of the technology revolution, it is difficult to have much perspective on its negative long-term impacts. To talk of its downside in the era of the Internet, the iPod, the BlackBerry, and cell phones in every woman's purse and hanging on every man's belt is to border on heresy. But technology's capacity to keep people wired twenty-four hours a day and to offer the distractions that undermine human conversations and interactions in a real, as opposed to a virtual, world is a fact that can't be ignored. Such intrusive devices can make people feel that there is no escape from work or from listening to strangers' unwanted one-sided communications.

I did one memorable study at a pharmaceutical company where people complained bitterly that they were inundated with information as they tried to carry out their sales calls to doctors not always anxious to give them an audience. The only time they had to catch up with the cascade of messages was after hours, when they were expected by family members to be fully present both mentally and physically. Worse, they didn't dare ignore the unwanted messages for fear they would miss something important regarding their work. It takes a rare person to resist the siren-like call of the handheld device.

A Pitney Bowes study conducted with the Institute for the Future in 2000 showed that the average person received and processed something like 178 messages a day from such devices as well as from official and unofficial sources and drop-in visits by coworkers.[1] Of those 178 messages, at least two or three were likely to take them off in a totally different direction from the one they anticipated when they began work that morning. A typical day in the office for that average office worker meant handling fifty-two phone calls, thirty-six emails, sixteen voicemails, twenty-three items posted on the company intranet, eight interoffice memos, fourteen faxes, and nine mobile phone calls. I'm convinced that if the study were replicated today, the multiplier effect from recent technological improvements would show the situation as much worse.

Obviously, we need to find ways to tame this kind of information overload. But so far we don't seem to be having a whole lot of success. The most promising strategies seem to be individually based, with people learning how to protect themselves from unwanted information using a variety of personal strategies based on either hasty inspection and deletion or some form of technological intervention to restrict and control the flow of information.

Consider a recent British study of how much time European managers are spending just on emails.[2] According to the study, by researchers at Henley College in the UK, European managers are spending two hours a day dealing with emails. The study's authors calculate that that adds up to a staggering ten years of a worker's life!

Of that number, three and a half years are seen as a complete waste of time because 32 percent of the messages are deemed irrelevant by their recipients. The cause—which, to be fair, is out of the control of communication professionals—is that each email message typically spawns four to six additional ones in the user's inbox.

A different kind of cost was shown in a psychological study of the impact of excessive attention to internet and other technology that allows people to stay connected. Carnegie Mellon randomly chose 169 people and tracked their internet behavior over one to two years. The assumption was that the increased connectivity would be good for their psychological health as they interacted with more and more people and experienced a richer range of social relationships than were available face-to-face.

Perversely, the researchers found just the opposite. It turned out that the more time people remained connected, the more depressed and isolated they felt.

The researchers' final hypothesis was that the subjects were building shallow virtual relationships that led to less connection with the real people around them. Their conclusion? Relationships over long distances without face-to-face connection ultimately don't provide the kind of reciprocity and support that contribute to well-being and a sense of psychological security or happiness.

Technology, Information, and Role Definition

One of the most important upsides of technology innovation for communication professionals has been the fulfillment of two wishes that many of my colleagues have cherished for years. The first is the ability to emulate the public media and to deliver unfiltered news to our employee public almost instantly. The second is the ability to open up the communication environment and provide for a more democratic information exchange between leadership and employees and, laterally as well, among employees.

Years ago I labeled that first wish and the desire to emulate the public media *reactive communication* because it is always a reaction to an event or new development. It is news reporting, clear and simple. No event, no new development = no communication. This *who, what, when, where,* and *why* approach was the fervent wish of the reactive communicators. Except that it was long on the first few w's and extremely short on the why. And it was frequently stopped in its tracks by timid and convoluted approval systems.

In a stable world, that was relatively harmless stuff. In a world changing chaotically, it was and is extremely dangerous, because it requires the audience to assemble bits of raw information and draw its own conclusions about meaning, leadership motives, and the why of the event. In my view it also flies in the face of the need to inform and educate—a need I regard as the most important mission of the internal communication professional.

In the last twenty or so years many companies have taken a dim view of reactive communication and made their communication strategies *proactive*, basing them instead on the creative and repetitive communication of business issues. Their goal was an informed employee public who understood the market forces that inevitably shaped the business strategies of their companies. Such a public, they believed, was better equipped to cope with the chaos of deep change and more likely to support the business goals.

Ironically, the technology explosion has brought reactive communication back into fashion. Intranets, like the Internet, thrive on sound-bite communication. They do an excellent job of delivering news and are superb in providing archives for company information. What they don't do—any more than the public media does—is to encourage quiet and thoughtful analysis, reflection, and clear thinking. In today's harried workplace the emphasis is increasingly on speed of delivery, sound bites, and instant judgments.

Here communication professionals are faced with another interesting and important role choice. Are they going to conceive of that role literally as a reporter/journalist/media specialist working inside the organization *or* as a surrogate for their leadership: advocating company positions, developing content, and educating the workforce to company realities? Most corporate leaders would clearly opt for the latter role, but a surprising number of communication professionals increasingly see themselves as a countervailing force operating almost like the independent news reporter, simply communicating the facts and leaving the conclusions to the audience.

The risk is a workforce that is actually less informed at work and less educated about their company or organization than they need to be in a competitive world. Consider the following statistics reported by leadership expert Stephen R. Covey from a poll of twenty-three thousand employees in a variety of organizations.[3]

- Only 37 percent say they had a clear understanding of what their organization is trying to achieve and why.
- Only 20 percent were enthusiastic about their team's and their organization's goals.
- 20 percent had a clear line of sight between their jobs and the organization's goals.
- 15 percent felt they were empowered or enabled to execute key goals.
- And only 20 percent trusted the leadership they work for.

Those are depressing comments on our effort to create an informed employee public. Worse, in the Information Age, they are indicators of a lack of context that inevitably inhibits our ability to contribute effectively to the organization's goals and priorities.

Covey goes on to say that if this were a football team, of eleven players:

- Only two players would be trying their hardest to win.
- Seven players would be somewhat interested in winning.
- And two players would actually be trying to help the other team win.

How likely would you be to bet on this team in any serious competition?

Technology, Social Media, and Information Democracy

The second wish of many communication professionals, as noted, has been to bring greater democracy and openness to the internal communication process. But this noble goal tends to clash with the authoritarian tendencies of most institutional organizations. In general, we still live in organizations that are autocratic and hierarchical in nature. The need for accountability and efficient decision making in business and other institutional organizations probably makes that reality inevitable, to a large extent, despite the wish for more democracy and openness.

The phenomenon that gives encouragement and hope to those who argue for more open corporate cultures is the so-called social media. No discussion of information and technology would be complete without addressing this phenomenon and the emerging movement to make it a prominent feature of corporate internal communication strategy. At this writing this is one of the most discussed trends in corporate or internet communication. Websites like MySpace, Facebook, YouTube, and an infinite number of blogs are fast becoming the staples of the

Internet as part of a phenomenon dubbed Web 2.0. Many communication professionals are moving to create internal company versions of these internet features as part of the regular social fabric of corporate life, as well as to spice up lifeless company intranets.

Social media includes, lumped together under this amorphous title, all sorts of communication channels, from personal blogs to wikis to message boards. Wikipedia, that online encyclopedia to which people voluntarily add uncensored definitions and descriptions, defines social media as "the online technologies and practices that people use to share opinions, insights, experiences and perspectives with each other." The definition goes on to say that popular social media include blogs, message boards, podcasts, wikis, and video podcasts. That obviously is one huge chunk of electronic territory.

It strikes me as wrongheaded to lump all of these together as though their common ability to facilitate dialogue makes them simply subcategories of the same species. It also complicates any examination of their usefulness. In truth, each one is essentially different from the others and has its own peculiar strengths and weaknesses. For example, blogs are virtual conversations posted electronically on the Internet or, increasingly, on company intranets. They are vehicles for anyone to express personal views for an undesignated and unseen group of online readers, who are urged to comment on the value of what they are reading and reply as they see fit in a continuing conversation.

Their virtue is their ability to connect people in dialogue about subjects they care deeply about. Their internet popularity is unprecedented, with an estimated population of seventy million or more bloggers worldwide. One could reasonably ask, who has the time to read all of this? But that misses the point. If two or more people are connected in meaningful conversations online, the blog has done its job.

Wikis are electronic "places" where communities of like-minded workers or thinkers can exchange ideas. Their value is in their constructive attempts to further the state of knowledge about a given subject or problem. Procter & Gamble and many other companies have provided wikis where people inside—or even outside the organization, in the case of P&G—can share ideas about a given problem or solution. The motivation for P&G to include outsiders is to widen its access to the best minds out there for solving their product issues and problems. In short, it's an initiative to broaden the conversation and to search for marketable, profitable ideas. And it's beautifully matched to the needs of the information assembly line and the networked organization. Given the need for this kind of information exchange among work teams and their members, there's a good chance that wikis have an important role to play in future internal communications.

The familiar message boards are well-known devices to allow varied groups of people to carry on extensive dialogue around common topics of interest—primarily on the Internet, although some companies are now offering message boards to various employee interest groups using their intranets. Podcasts are radio or video productions that can be downloaded by interested listeners and viewers and played back at their convenience, an obvious advantage in a highly pressured, time-starved environment—especially when people are spread out geographically.

Corporate Democracy and Social Media

Social media are capturing the imagination of communication professionals as have few developments in the profession. They are seen by their proponents as a means of introducing greater democracy in organizations and undercutting the arbitrary power of senior people. Much is made of that point. An important motivation of those who advocate employee blogs, in particular, is the urge to make communication and information delivery less top-down and to dilute executive authority and hierarchy. Their objective is to make the institutional organization a more democratic place, with lively dialogue resembling that found on the Internet.

The logic goes something like this: it's a new age in which today's worker is demanding the right to self expression. Such expression, it's claimed, will promote a freer and richer social climate in which people get to connect with and to know their peers better while sharing both information and views inside and outside the company. The obvious virtue of such media inside a company is that they permit the sharing of information horizontally as well as vertically. Their proponents claim that they are also more in tune with today's networked organization, in which information must move across functions if the organization is to operate efficiently. The argument is also made that the upcoming so-called Generation Y will demand nothing less than the right to free expression and continuous contact with their peers—a circumstance that has typified most of their young lives.

The tandem evolution of technology and social media in recent years in this Web 2.0 world has provided unprecedented opportunities for people to broadcast their views and ideas without the usual gatekeepers, who could improve, censor, or even decline to allow their distribution. Thus everyone now has the capability to be both author and publisher.

And to the advocates, that's one of their great advantages. Their assertion is that the public media, and by extension corporate internal media, are corrupt, arrogant, slanted, and deeply biased in one direction or another and can't be trusted. Social media are the antidote because they permit anyone to become a reporter or observer without the editing and fact checking of traditional media. It is inclusion, democracy, and free speech to the nth degree, based on the notion that the people should have their say—a noble idea clearly rooted in our traditions of free speech and belief in the wisdom of the people.

But the expectation that people will police themselves and engage only in high-minded dialogue and not abuse the right and privilege of open communication is proving to be a bit naive. To their collective discomfort, the public media are beginning to learn that lesson from seeing too many uncivil, scurrilous, and poorly considered reader blogs. In their rush to embrace blogging as a means of combating declining circulation, they forgot to figure out how to monitor and, where necessary, even censor inappropriate comment. (For more on that subject, see Andrew Keen's polemic *The Cult of the Amateur: How Today's Internet Is Killing Our Culture.*)

The other negative of social media is that it has the ability to bury us with even more information overload and to distract us from the important information we need to live, survive, and succeed in a complicated and changing environment. In the process it can ultimately dilute and drive out good communication with excessive amounts of bad communication—that which is poorly conceived, largely irrelevant to the business, and indiscriminately delivered.

Further, without proper and careful controls it can expose companies to serious potential legal issues that no one can really predict at this point. A survey reported in the publication *Strategic Communication Management* shows that 39 percent of those who kept blogs admitted posting potentially sensitive company information or information that could be damaging to their organizations, employer, or colleagues.

And then there is the productivity concern, as people spend valuable work time on matters that may have little to do with their job responsibilities. Most companies take a dim view of distractions that interfere with the work effort. Finally, excessive attention to social media can also tempt us to abdicate our responsibility to create and execute thoughtful communication strategies in favor of simply promoting and facilitating free-form dialogue—dialogue that inevitably increases the noise level in our organizations.

Finding what is valuable in this complex mix and resisting the temptation to mindlessly follow the crowd in its uncritical acceptance is a serious challenge we need to consider thoughtfully and with due regard for a solid, balanced communication strategy.

Preparing the Way for Gen Y

Among the positions that the enthusiasts of social media are taking is their interesting generational argument that social media are so essential to the needs and habits of Generation Y—that huge cohort now in varying stages of development from kindergarten to entry-level jobs—that they must be adopted in the workplace. Without this capability to connect with their peers, some observers argue, Gen Yers will either decline to join large organizations or simply ignore any prohibitions placed on social media at work. In the worst case they will reject those job opportunities and those organizational cultures that seem disinterested in adjusting to their ingrained habits of connection.

The specter of intergenerational conflict is often raised in this discussion as people observe that the baby boom generation and Generation X, the generation in between the boomers and Gen Y, operate from a different value system and different work habits. The baby boomers are stereotyped as corporate-loyal and willing to do what the boss says. That's ironic for a generation that was determined enough to protest and end a war, stage a social revolution against repressive sexual mores, and figuratively blow pot smoke in the faces of their astonished and worried elders. Adding to the stereotypes, the Gen Xers are "pragmatic, free-agent types with scrappy personalities." Gen Y members, on the other hand, are stereotyped as having high expectations and believing that they are special. In addition, it is said they are enthusiastic, have good attitudes, and want to be challenged as well as coached, mentored, and respected.

Les Potter, a well-known communication practitioner and instructor at Towson University in Maryland, notes that as this generation—born in 1982 and later—enters the workforce, they will necessarily be working with and for those generational groups who preceded them. He accurately observes that how they relate to the other generational groups will determine their success or failure. He adds that, conversely, the way in which those groups relate to the Gen Y people will determine who recruits and retains the best and the brightest of them. A future Bill Gates could certainly be quickly turned off by a boss with a smothering, autocratic style.

Such stereotypes aside, there is no doubt that possible generational conflict in information-sharing habits and personal styles of consuming information may well cause problems. The Gen Y members, also known as Millennials, face an interesting set of challenges if they opt to join large corporate organizations. For one thing, middle-aged and older workers, proud of their own experience and accomplishments, may well feel somewhat threatened by the technical skills possessed by the Gen Y cohort and fearful about being "shown up" by younger workers. There may also be a conflict regarding the alleged Gen Y desire to be viewed as "special" in cultures which often are long on criticism of individuals and short on recognition. A generation raised by so-called "helicopter parents" may find themselves more on their own than they may like and faced—fairly or unfairly— with some skepticism about the likelihood of their making vital contributions so early in their experience with the companies that employ them. Still, the organizations that need their skills are, for the most part, anxious to welcome them and to tap their impressive technical talents.

Other than the coming of the baby boomers, there has rarely been such discussion and preparation for any generation entering corporate life. Doubtless, much of that preparation has to do with the aging baby boomer workforce and the reality that they will be retiring in unprecedented numbers in the coming years. The business literature is full of advice on how to understand Gen Yers and their needs and to welcome them in such a way that they will grow into productive and talented contributors.

But most organizations are fond of forcing some degree of conformity and assimilation onto people new to their cultures. The prevailing view has always been that newcomers must fig-ure out the norms and adapt their behavior to the prevailing standards. Here is where the potential generational clash lies, if we are to accept the stereotype that the Gen Yers are and were a watched-over generation whose parents protected them and obsessed over them at every age. The other part of the ste-reotype is that they have a close and friendly relationship with those parents, almost on a peer-to-peer basis as they've grown up. Of course, all of this smacks of middle- and upper-middle-class values and, like all stereotypes, may be grossly misleading when applied to any individual.

To the extent that it's accurate, however, the members of Gen Y may be in for some rude shocks when they enter the likes of a General Motors, an Exxon, or even a Cisco or Microsoft. In the last two companies the cultures may be a bit more tolerant of the young contributor who expects to be recognized as special and to be carefully mentored in his or her career. This might happen in such organizations, but in many others there will be some painful adjustments on both sides of any generation gap.

If asked, the advice I plan to give to the Millennials in my own family will be to play it cool, to not expect special treat-ment, and to display a fair amount of humility about how much they have to learn from those who have weathered the storms of organizational life. In the team-oriented cultures that are typical in most organizations today, I will tell them, they will probably feel some degree of comfort and welcome, but, like everyone else, they will have to earn respect over time by performing, contributing selflessly, and otherwise paying their dues.

Another important lesson is that organizations expect per-sonal discipline and productivity from the people they employ. To ignore those expectations is to court trouble. They should expect considerable disapproval if they spend their work time exploring favorite sites on the Internet or socializing excessively with coworkers. We are still not that far removed from the old Industrial Revolution order in which supervisors walked the floors and checked the activity level, work, and work habits of the people they supervised. Regardless of what anyone may say to the contrary, activity, diligence, and punctuality are close to sacred values in organizations, and the appearance or absence of those virtues in any employee still counts for a great deal in judging performance.

On the other hand, I will tell my grandchildren that their impressive skills in manipulating technology and using information to create new products and services will serve them very well. To the extent that they are able to use those skills to teach, to innovate, and to perform, they will stand out and be recognized as people who, in the words of the corporate lexicon, add value. That's the real secret of corporate success.

And, if I happen to be in a preachy mood on the day of this imaginary conversation, I may remind them that their baby boomer parents and perhaps grandparents, who may now strike them as overly corporate and loyal, were once described as another generation that was going to dramatically alter the cultures of the organizations they joined. To some extent they did, but as the realities of global competition began to inflict real damage on once proud American industries like steel, office equipment manufacturing, automobiles, and the like, leaders of these and similarly embattled companies wheeled out the heavy artillery. They reminded the boomers that they could get along with far fewer of their numbers, and they downsized and early-retired them just when they were middle-aged, vulnerable, and short of options.

That wasn't a matter of revenge. It was more a question of facing what the game of business ultimately comes down to—costs, productivity, and profits. Perhaps General Electric CEO Jeffrey Immelt said it best. In an interview with USA Today he was asked to comment on Gen Y and their expectations. After noting just how talented they were and what impressive technical skills they would bring to the party as a generation, he added a warning: they have to remember, however, that in India and China there is a talented Generation A who want the same things young Westerners already have. That is the competitive reality that must temper their expectations.

Summing Up: Information and the Communication Professional

So where do we wind up on this important question of the power and potential of information and its role in today's organization? The challenge for the communication profession is to determine how to use and manage information thoughtfully and efficiently and to deliver it properly to a skeptical audience—an audience already drowning in raw information in a time-pressured world where they are often stretched close to the breaking point. We need to be cautious about adding to that deluge of raw information as opposed to information that has been tested for insight, truthfulness, accuracy, and value.

Technology, with all of its profound advantages, has opened up a Pandora's box and revolutionized the way we interact in organizations and the ways in which we will do business going forward. It has also raised expectations as well as perplexing questions about the proper role of the internal communication professional in relating to it and to effective information management and delivery.

Perhaps, as we will examine in the next chapter, the mitigating factor that will allow us to manage both information and technology appropriately will be the business and human needs of its users. That's the real goal we should be pursuing.

3

NEEDS ON THE JOB

Whatever else we can say about the communication process in organizations, it's clear that in the final analysis it's all about people and what they need and want to know. That sounds so obvious that it should not need to be pointed out, but it's amazing how often human needs for communication in organizations are ignored.

Truthful and effective communication requires, above all, an understanding of the audience. All communication strategy and tactics should focus on, as a first cause, what information the audience wants and needs. For anyone who cares to look, there's plenty of standing data on what kind of communication employees need if they are going to be productive and engaged.

In truth, it all comes down to the rather simple formula I offered earlier. Where is the organization going? How does it propose to get there? And what does it all mean to *me*? Why that is so is not hard to figure out. People want predictability, and they want to know the likely prospects of the company as well as the degree of personal security they might reasonably expect.

A Landmark Set of Findings

One of the most interesting studies ever done in this regard was conducted some years ago at Texas Instruments, as reported by a TI industrial engineering executive named Earl Gommersall. He and his colleagues were looking for ways to entice manufacturing production employees to become more involved in what at the time was called *participative management* (today it would be given the label *employee engagement*). The simple objective was to get more of the employees' discretionary effort and ideas and experience to influence innovation and successful production.

A group of academicians had worked with TI to determine what it would take to help make manufacturing workers more involved in their work and more engaged generally. In the end, they concluded that TI assembly line workers had three basic needs on the job. The first was for *job mastery*: they needed to get to a reasonable comfort level where they felt they understood what was expected of them and believed that they met those essential requirements. In a word, they wanted to achieve competence.

Once they believed that they had job mastery, their next need was for *predictability*: if I do thus and so, this is the likely consequence. Under normal circumstances on the job it took lots of time for them to figure out the predictable responses to their behavior, as much of it was a matter of trial and error. *If I make a mistake, here's how the boss is likely to react. If I am often absent from work, I may get reprimanded, put on probation, or fired.* And on and on until they had tested the organization's likely responses to their positive or negative behavior.

After they had achieved a reasonable level of job mastery and predictability, they manifested a much higher human need. They wanted to be recognized for their *contributions*. The researchers then revised that finding and upped the ante. They said that it was more than a desire for recognition. What the people in the study really wanted was *to be loved*. To TI's credit, although it must have caused some consternation in a macho manufacturing environment, they didn't flinch at this finding. This aspiration, of course, was set in the era of long-term employment and job security predating the massive waves of downsizing that typified the 1980s and '90s and that continues well into the twenty-first century.

If employees reached the point at which they felt that they were indeed loved—that is, they were recognized as highly valued members of the organization—the researchers found these same employees had a reciprocal need to love back. At this point they were at last willing to go the extra mile and actually participate wholeheartedly in their work.

It was a fascinating set of findings and insight into not only what made the TI worker feel engaged but also what forces motivate most of us, to one degree or another, at work.

At the time, Gommersall and his associates took advantage of the findings to speed up the kinds of socialization that would tend to engage their workforce. One interesting innovation was the introduction of predictability seminars, in which new employees were not only given extensive job training to make sure their skills were adequate but were also told of the elements of the job they otherwise would have had to discover on their own. For example, they were informed that the electronic welders they would be using would likely result in minor burns no matter how careful they were. They were also given profiles of their bosses—their likes and dislikes and leadership styles— much as athletes would get a scouting report before a big game.

All of this was a calculated effort to meet the human needs of the workforce for predictability before they set foot in their assigned areas. As a result, they adapted to their work much more quickly and easily than those who had not been given this kind of orientation. Other types of leadership and communication innovations—like team meetings, listening sessions, breakfast meetings with management, and enhanced supervisory training— were also included to ensure that the employees got the kind of recognition and attention that the study had shown they craved. Productivity and levels of engagement soared as a result of the attention paid to worker needs.

Supervisory attitudes also underwent a serious change. After Gommersall made it clear that he expected his supervisors to communicate more effectively about the business and its issues, he often recounted, with amusement, that it wasn't uncommon to see an employee from the line on his way to a breakfast meeting with his boss running beside him saying, "And don't forget to tell him what I told you about . . . " The overall impact on the work climate from the new understandings and recognition was impressive. Since those days numerous other studies have in their own way replicated the essential TI findings.

Gallup and Employee Engagement

In much more recent and deeper research, Marcus Buckingham, when he was part of the Gallup Organization, reported essentially the same thing in different but somewhat similar terms. In his fascinating book *First, Break All the Rules* he outlines the underpinnings of Gallup's important work on employee engagement.[4] In 1998 Gallup deliberately set out to measure what they called "strong" workplaces—those that would attract and hold the best and most competent workers. They selected twenty-four different companies in a cross section of twelve different industries to test four different business outcomes: productivity, profitability, employee retention, and customer satisfaction. Ultimately, over one hundred thousand employees took part.

Buckingham and Gallup concluded from their study that some twelve questions could measure the strength of a workplace and the level of what they called "employee engagement." In summary, they found that every one of the twelve questions linked to at least one of the four outcomes they were seeking. For example, ten of the twelve questions linked to the productivity measure. Eight showed a link to profitability. And five showed a link to retention.

In reviewing their findings, the researchers identified the following six questions as having the strongest links to the most positive business outcomes:

1. Do I know what's expected of me at work?
2. Do I have the materials and equipment I need to do my work right?

3. Do I have the opportunity to do what I do best every day?

4. In the last seven days, have I received recognition or praise for good work?

5. Does my supervisor, or someone at work, seem to care about me as a person?

6. Is there someone at work who encourages my development?

   The balance of what came to be known as the Q12 questions was as follows:

7. At work, do my opinions seem to count?

8. Does the mission/purpose of my company make me feel my job is important?

9. Are my coworkers committed to doing quality work?

10. Do I have a best friend at work?

11. In the last six months, has someone talked to me about my progress?

12. This last year, have I had opportunities at work to learn and grow?

Interestingly, the researchers concluded that the single influence that made the most difference in the degree of employee engagement was the behavior of the person's immediate manager. In fact, if you look at those first six questions, they are all about the relationship with that manager and his or her ability to satisfy employee needs. That's a critical cue for communication professionals, the vast majority of whom typically have tended to ignore that relationship as beyond their charters or skills.

The reality is that if the supervisory relationship is broken, the employee "hears" nothing else that is communicated to him or her. It literally falls on deaf ears. People pay the greatest attention to the conditions closest to their immediate environments, the places where they live their work lives. The ultimate lesson of the Gallup research is this: what we commonly call "face-to-face communication," regardless of all of the other novel communication techniques we discover, will remain the most critical and effective communication technique (more about that in the next chapter).

If you look at the Q12, you will soon see that most formalized organizational communication efforts are directed squarely at the satisfaction of question 8, namely: Does the mission/purpose of my company make me feel my job is important? It's important that this is one of the twelve questions of engagement, but it is only one. The other eleven are usually left to the leadership style and values of the individual company managers, with little or no accountability for the kind of behavior that the questions assert are crucial to employee needs and, therefore, to the achievement of the company's business goals. It's a mind-boggling omission.

More Evidence

Although the Gallup research is far more rigorous than what TI had reported earlier, notice how that earlier research foreshadows the Gallup findings. It's all about caring for employee needs. Veteran survey expert David Sirota provides further evidence of the real communication and leadership needs of employees on the job, summarizing more than thirty years of employee research that he and his firm conducted.[5] His findings generally parallel those of the Gallup Q12 research, but he expresses them according to three critical measures—achievement, fair treatment, and relationships at work—all of which lead to an overall employee satisfaction measure.

According to his norms, what he terms "a company of enthusiastic employees" (roughly equivalent to the Gallup vision of employee engagement) must meet a criterion of 75 percent of its employees declaring positive overall morale and no more than 10 percent indicating dissatisfaction. Morale is measured on a continuum of four levels: enthusiasm, satisfaction, neutrality, and anger. Demonstrating the rigor of this standard, only 13.8 percent of the included companies rate as having an enthusiastic work-force. Most important, there is a strong correlation between high levels of enthusiasm and business success. That, of course, is always the golden measure: do such findings translate to bottom-line results?

My own experience resonates with the Sirota and Gallup findings. In my years of listening to and researching employ-ees in all kinds of organizations, I've observed several critical employee needs: the need to be recognized for one's achieve-ments, the desire to be valued for one's inherent worth, the need to be part of something worth belonging to, and the need for social interaction in a compatible community of coworkers in which fairness is a recognized and supported value.

In the Texas Instruments example, the most basic need was for "job mastery"—that sense that one can do this work com-petently and with some level of comfort. It's what we all strive for—the feeling of satisfaction from accomplishment. Its oppo-site feeling—a sense of failure and inability to perform—is one of the most demotivating human experiences. Ironically, the all-too-common tendency in organizations is to dwell on someone's deficiencies and shortcomings when measuring performance. We tend to be good fault finders but not very good at recogniz-ing and praising accomplishment.

One of the most common laments I hear from people in the workplace has to do with lack of recognition for hard work and accomplishment. I've always thought much of that goes back to bad parenting—either from the way we ourselves were raised, with overly critical parents, or the style of parenting we person-ally find most comfortable.

I don't mean to suggest that the supervisor or manager is or should be in a parental role. That's demeaning for the person being supervised, and anyway there has been far too much of that thinking and behavior in organizations in the past. Adults need to be treated like adults if we are to expect adult behavior. But it's difficult for us to escape that simple notion of authority, punishment, and the withholding of praise, because the models of "bossism" as opposed to leadership are so prevalent in our world.

That tendency to want to point out shortcomings in evaluating performance without sufficient attention to accomplishment is one of the reasons that so few people find performance evaluations a satisfying or useful experience. Many people who wind up in supervisory or managerial positions have a difficult time providing fair and balanced feedback to people. Either they shy away from communicating performance shortcomings for fear of offending the people they manage, or they withhold praise for fear of causing people to rest on their laurels and feel that there is little to strive for. One of the common manipulative techniques for managing people is to always keep them wondering and off balance, looking for the approval they rarely get from such managers.

Whether we want to acknowledge it or not in tough-minded organizations, people do indeed have a need to be loved—or at least valued and respected at work. It's depressing to see the enthusiastic and ambitious new worker coming into an organization, ready to contribute and achieve, only to see that same person a year later, discouraged and worn down by an ineffective boss who doesn't have a clue about leading people effectively. The old rejoinder from those who have trouble recognizing performance tells it all. "That's why we give them a paycheck."

Gallup's Q12 questions 5 and 6 make the point: Does my supervisor, or someone at work, seem to care about me as a person? Is there someone at work who encourages my development? Those are the needs that, when they go unmet, tend to turn off the otherwise motivated worker.

Beyond this need to be valued, fairness and community are also vital employee needs in the workplace. When you ask people who for one reason or another are dissatisfied and disengaged at work why they stay, the answer is usually one or more variations on the same theme: "The money and benefits are good, and I like the people I work with." Sometimes they go on to offer more specific reasons, like "the timing is wrong to leave a secure job" or "I love this area where I grew up, and I don't want to leave my extended family" or "I don't have the education or experience to try something else" or a variety of other explanations of why they stay. But the most common reasons come down to that notion of a predictable and secure, if not necessarily satisfying, job and the opportunity to work with people they like. It seems all too often that the human condition dictates a "better the devil you know" mentality as opposed to uncertainty and risk-taking. One memorable example of this behavior in my own experience was a focus group I was conducting at an automotive plant. A particularly upset older woman was lamenting the ineffectiveness of management, the inequity of the pay, the constant threats of downsizing, and a long list of other shortcomings. Before I could ask her why she stayed with the company, she leveled her final complaint, with no sense of irony: "And the thing that really upsets me is that my son can't get a job here."

To those who would counter that the paycheck is enough and that employee satisfaction is nice but not that important, I offer another study, conducted by the Medill Integrated Marketing Communications (IMC) graduate program at Northwestern University. In a study of one hundred organizations in the U.S. media industry, the researchers concluded that there is a direct relationship among employee satisfaction, customer satisfaction, and improved financial performance.[6] Further, the key organizational characteristic for explaining satisfaction, they said, is a measure of downward and upward communication effectiveness in an organization. Their findings also supported Buckingham's conclusion that the critical relationship in determining both satisfaction and the degree of employee engagement is that between an employee and his or her manager.

Commonality

What's interesting is the commonality in all of these findings. Intelligent communication professionals need to study such data and ensure that their counsel and their various strategies are consistent with the well-documented human needs on the job.

In particular, that requires careful attention to communication as the holistic and dynamic process it really is in the workplace. It's not simply internal journalism; it's attention to a process that is closely allied with the entire issue of organizational leadership and the requirement to lead people responsibly and effectively if we want results.

One of my favorite clients notes that the tendency in most organizations has been to undertake what she calls an "SOS" communication strategy—sending out stuff. Obviously, such a strategy is attractive because it makes leaders and communication professionals alike believe that they are doing something tangible to address their various communication challenges. The trouble is, that's a scatter-gun approach to a set of needs that are very clear if one is willing to look at them objectively. Some years ago a former Xerox colleague of mine likened this strategy to wetting yourself in a dark suit. His follow-up line was, "No one notices, and it makes you feel warm all over."

Too many of my colleagues see organizational communication strictly as a media-based enterprise. As respected British consultant Bill Quirke puts it, they revel in the journey, whereas their leaders care most deeply about arriving at the destination. He adds, "The leaders play by 'big boy and girl rules' while communication professionals love the journey." In short, the communication professionals tend to love communication craft, whereas their organizations are primarily interested in outcomes—understanding, behavior change, and a greater likelihood of an engaged workforce.

Determining Needs in Your Organization

The universal truths reported in these various studies of employee needs beg the question of what people want and need in your own organization. To get at that critical issue, you need to do the kind of data gathering that will augment what the standing employee research tells us.

The best data gathering is done face-to-face with two groups—the leadership of your company and the employees themselves. How do you get started? I think the beginning point is a good old-fashioned sit-down interview with each of the senior leaders in your organization. The objective is to find out what communication issues are on their collective minds and to see how they match up with what employees want to know about. The details of how to do that kind of research are summarized in Chapter Six.

Employee Engagement

One of the most cherished of leadership outcomes is a more engaged workforce. Why that is so in a highly competitive global environment is no mystery. Competitive organizations depend on people who are willing to go the extra mile, to give more than the average worker is willing to invest at work. Figuring out how to increase the extent of employee engagement in any organization should be one of the most important agenda items for the professional communicator. There is no question that human communication and engagement go hand in hand. Indeed, without proper attention to the communication aspects of engagement, there is little hope of creating that enthusiastic workforce that is so critical to performance and business success.

Towers Perrin, one of the most respected human resource consulting organizations, has done extensive research to identify what they call the drivers of employee engagement. In a global study of eighty-six thousand employees around the world, they identified some important insights into what tends to persuade people to engage.[7] The data show that worldwide only about 14 percent of employees rate themselves as "highly engaged," with an equal number stating that they are actually "disengaged." That latter group is usually made up of those jaded employees who pull aside the newcomers and begin their unofficial mentoring with "Hey, kid, let me tell you how things really work around here."

Those engagement numbers leave about 72 percent of the working population who are moderately engaged or, as Towers Perrin describes them, "willing but wary." Obviously there is a huge potential upside opportunity to increase those sorry levels of engagement by doing the right thing by employees.

What is that right thing? TP divides the items that define engagement into two categories—what they term the emotional factors and the rational ones. The emotional ones come down to the following survey items, which are defined as *inspiration* and *aspiration*:

- I really care about the future of my organization.
- I am proud to tell others I work for my organization.
- My job provides me with a sense of personal accomplishment.
- I would recommend my organization to a friend as a good place to work.
- My organization inspires me to do my best work.

The so-called rational factors have to do with the individual's relationship with the organization. Those survey items show that understanding leads to a desire to go the extra mile.

- I understand how my unit/department contributes to the success of my organization.
- I understand how my role in the organization is related to my organization's overall goals, objectives, and direction.
- I am willing to put in a great deal of effort beyond what is normally expected to help my organization succeed.
- I am personally motivated to help my organization be successful.

In analyzing the results, the Towers Perrin researchers identified the elements they believe it takes to create a more engaged workforce. The first critical element is a visible senior leadership team. Employees need to see and hear their leaders. They also want to understand the organization's vision, mission, and goals, as well as how their efforts and work fit into that scheme. And they also want to believe that their leadership is honest and candid in its dealings with them.

The second element is dedication to learning, skill enhancement, and career development. Many organizations have greatly improved their efforts at training and development, but in my personal experience they have a long way to go on the issue of career development. Most companies I see send employees the message that career development is up to them. That's not a very helpful stance in a confusing and chaotically changing world. It may make sense as a principle, but in practice it leaves the average employee without guidance or proper feedback on his or her prospects.

The third element is effective frontline management and supervision. The fact is that people quit bad bosses, not organizations. This is a primary communication relationship that shouldn't be left merely to chance and the supervisor's personal style. Training, tools, and accountability measures are all important factors in addressing this issue. More about that in the next chapter.

The fourth element in creating a more engaged workforce is a well-thought-out and equitable reward strategy that is also well communicated and effectively implemented. Such a strategy must be based on an understanding of what people value and what rewards tend to motivate them to greater levels of performance.

Finally, the fifth element: people want to work for a company that has a solid reputation as an employer. Interestingly, this factor came through in every country in the survey. It's a normal human desire to be associated with a winner, with worthwhile and admirable causes and organizations. Somehow that association makes one feel more important as a member of a group worth belonging to.

If you look carefully at all of this research, it is clear that much of it is based on effective human communication and relationship. When Gommersall and his associates at TI posited the human need to be loved and the need to love back as a precondition of engagement, they were right on the money.

The actual report cards on how well both senior and front-line management are doing against the engagement criteria are not very encouraging. For example, in an earlier (2000) Towers Perrin survey of North American workers, senior leaders got only 37 percent favorable scores on open and honest communication, 47 percent on integrity, and 45 percent on a clear vision for success.

Similarly, supervisors received a score of only 43 percent on overall effectiveness. Their best scores for aspects of this were for supporting teamwork and integrity, at 59 percent and 58 percent, respectively. They received poorer scores on encouraging new ideas and providing clear direction—49 percent. And their lowest scores were 46 percent for inspiring enthusiasm. At that, their overall scores topped those of their senior leaders. Clearly, in this case organizational distance does not make the heart grow fonder. In fact, leaders who are invisible and inaccessible tend to create trust issues with their people—not a surprising fact.

The Art of the Possible

One remaining question is, how much engagement is truly possible in any organization? When researchers analyze self-appraisals of who is highly engaged, moderately engaged, and disengaged, across the board the usual responses hover around 15, 70, and 15 percent. Can this perennial proportion be improved?

I have a personal theory that engagement, in the final analysis, is essentially an individual choice that is exercised day by day and maybe even hour by hour in the work day. So to speak of engagement levels as though they were static and a macro rather than a micro issue misses the point. The real action is at the personal relationship level. I doubt that most of us have the capacity to maintain ever higher levels of personal employee engagement at work. And I'm pretty sure that engagement is highly dependent on the human relationships closest to us at work.

That doesn't mean we shouldn't pursue this objective as diligently as we possibly can at both the company and the individual level. Too often the matter is dismissed as a "soft issue" we can't get hold of. In truth it is one of the "hardest" issues that any of us could imagine—in terms of both its importance to performance and the difficulty of achievement.

But think of the potential prize for the organization that can find ways to move its workforce from "willing but wary" to engaged for a good share of the available work time. The potential productivity and overall performance gains from such movement with a possible three-quarters of the workforce are incredible.

Towers Perrin, in its final conclusions on engagement and other related issues, offers a realistic view of those difficulties:

"In today's flattening world, there's no question that companies will find it harder to meet these challenges. And there's no question that meeting them successfully is more critical than ever . . . Companies that have begun the work of building the right framework—one that rests on the elements outlined above—will be far better positioned to adapt themselves to a flat world." And that is the game that is most worth playing.

Implications for Communication Professionals

I can well imagine some communication professionals reading this and saying to themselves, *Those are issues for human resource people to worry about; they're not really my concern.* I couldn't disagree more. In my view these are the real needs that should both determine our various communication strategies and dictate the tactics we use to address those needs. Communication is a robust and dynamic process based largely on human relationships and intelligent leadership at all levels. It is fundamental to the successful functioning of the intellectual capital assembly line.

We should definitely worry about moving information effectively and seeking understanding and support for the organization's goals and objectives. But if we ignore the real needs of our audience and insist on finding novel media and technological solutions to what are fundamental human issues, we will badly miss the mark—and our organizations and the people they comprise will pay for our neglect.

4

FACE-TO-FACE

The Irving Berlin classic immortalized by Fred Astaire and Ginger Rogers goes "Heaven, I'm in heaven . . . when we're out together dancing cheek to cheek." In the communication world and in the world of work, that lyric could well be restated as "I'm in heaven . . . when we sit together talking face-to-face." Because we are social animals conditioned by millennia of evolutionary experiences, we tend to prefer the experience of face-to-face encounters, in which we can judge all sorts of familiar communication clues, such as the level and amount of eye contact, tone and timbre of voice, body language, and general demeanor. The visual and oral clues tell us whether the message is sincere or not and even whether we can trust the person delivering it and where and how we can join in the dialogue. It is an invaluable part of the human communication experience.

Practically all of the research indicates that the most preferred communication experience at work is live and face-to-face. This is particularly so in the relationship between the worker and his or her immediate supervisor. In fact, plenty of research confirms that when this relationship goes sour, most people are inclined to quit their jobs and their companies. Most exit interviews, if they are conducted honestly, reveal that the cause of the resignation has much to do with a bad boss's neglect of good face-to-face communication.

What does that kind of communication look like? We can all describe it from our personal experience. It is first of all respectful. None of us wants to be denigrated, screamed at, or belittled in a conversation. Second, it is open. We believe that, as long as we are courteous and calm, we should be able to say what's on our minds candidly without fear of retribution. The old saying that "they kill the messenger of bad news around here" in an organization casts a pall on all candor. A bitter observer of the communication climate in an organization where one of my daughters worked advised her, "Around here they don't want to hear your opinions. In fact, they'll shoot your ass off. So better to say nothing." Rarely have I heard the admonition expressed so clearly.

The third requirement is that the communication is nondefensive on the part of all parties. To achieve that desired state, an organization must be careful not to punish people when they deliver unwelcome news and to have the ability to listen without jumping automatically to a defense of their behavior.

Courtesy in organizations is sometimes in short supply, but it should go without saying that exchanges at work should be characterized by good manners. That means no quick dismissals of ideas or concerns and a constant respect for polite discourse. At an automotive plant where I was doing some consulting work, I once was told by some of the middle managers that a given plant manager was especially gruff, arbitrary, and discourteous in his treatment of subordinates. His abusive and unpredictable behavior with plant employees was legendary and a cause of constant fear. Their descriptions of his behavior were memorable. "You know the difference between our plant manager and Hitler?" they asked rhetorically. Without waiting for a response, they rushed to the punch line: "He lacks Hitler's warmth and compassion." Happily, that plant manager's behavior did not go unnoticed by his bosses, and he was eventually fired—but not before he had done considerable damage.

A final quality of the effective leader or manager is accessibility. In this day of pressured workplaces and managers that suffer from a lack of time to do their jobs properly, accessibility is often a problem. But the good ones find time to put aside the paperwork and get out of their offices to seek communication exchanges with the people for whom they are responsible.

During my time at Xerox, a survey was administered to permit employees to evaluate the effectiveness of their managers. Two bottom-line questions asked employees to rate the overall effectiveness of their manager and whether or not he or she would be regarded as a role model for other managers. One survey item was the absolute predictor of either favorable or unfavorable ratings on both counts: the manager's openness and accessibility.

One of the best examples of such an excellent leader in my own experience was a retired navy admiral named George Spaulding. He was the CEO of the small technology company where I was the communication manager in one of my first jobs. He was basically a rather shy man by nature, but he began every day by walking the company premises and deliberately engaging people in conversation. It was not an easy or comfortable task for him, but he felt that it was important to get out of his office and talk to and listen to people. In the beginning of his tenure as CEO they were all a bit intimidated and not especially comfortable asking him questions. But despite his years of military formality, he shed his coat and did everything he could to engage his initially reluctant listeners in conversation.

To make the process work more effectively, he asked his assistant to make sure that he had photos of all four hundred of the people who worked in the company. I sometimes saw him thumbing through the thick photo album, memorizing names and faces so that he could call people by name. He also made notes of any personal work or family employee issues that would help him better connect during his daily strolls. The result was that his workforce would have walked through fire for him.

When I was a consultant for Towers Perrin, we had an ongoing assignment at Perdue Farms, the chicken processor in Salisbury, Maryland. We were invited to work with groups of employees to help improve communication. My Towers Perrin colleague at the time, Jim Shaffer, had been asked by CEO and owner Frank Perdue to help set up an employee suggestion plan. Perdue had felt that such a plan would help boost morale and improve communication. When asked what he thought of the plan, Jim tactfully demurred and said that such plans work in some environments, but he didn't think that it was a very good idea here. Perdue persisted and asked him to come up with a plan or offer other alternatives to meet his objective. In the end, worker teams were established to offer their ideas of how to improve the communication climate.

By this time Perdue had become something of a celebrity, appearing in his own national television ads, in which he praised the quality and flavor of his chickens. The fact that he vaguely resembled a chicken was not lost on him, and he was willing to exploit it in his commercials. One of the employee teams noted that he was more visible on television than he was in the processing plant, and the members worked up the courage to send a delegation to tell him so. Their advice was simple: remove the suit jacket, loosen your tie, and come talk with us. To his great credit, he did exactly that, even taking their coaching on how he should behave and the subjects people were most interested in. The results of his willingness to listen to the team and take their coaching made for great strides in improving the internal communication climate.

Frontline Communication

These are examples of senior leadership and communication styles that work, but the most important and most neglected form of face-to-face communication is at the frontline level. I say most neglected because most organizations operate under the assumption that such frontline communication takes care of itself, and they leave it to the individual style and habits of each frontline manager. It's a dangerous practice for such an important activity as effective communication by those who lead the day-to-day operations of a company.

Writing in *First, Break All the Rules*, Marcus Buckingham emphasizes the critical leadership role of managers and supervisors and disagrees with the proposition that company policies are the main determinant of the effectiveness of a culture. Here's what he says:

"It's not that these employee-focused initiatives are unimportant. It's just that your immediate manager is *more* important. She defines and pervades your work environment. If she sets clear expectations, knows you, trusts you, and invests in you, you can forgive the company its lack of a profit sharing program . . . It's better to work for a great manager in an old-fashioned company than for a terrible manager in a company offering an enlightened, employee-focused culture."[8]

I have my own views of what makes that great manager great. It is the ability to address and answer six fundamental questions that tend to define the communication relationship between any employee and his or her manager. When I was with Xerox, I formulated these six questions while doing a study of why our managers and supervisors were not doing a more effective job of frontline communication. We knew from our extensive surveying that this was the case, and we wanted to know why. The company was enlightened. It hired the best and the brightest. We wanted to know why our managers and team leaders weren't managing that precious human resource in a way that satisfied their communication needs on the job.

I got the answers in one of the first interviews I did in New York City. I had sat down with the then-branch manager and had begun posing the neat set of questions we had put together when, in the middle of the interview, he reached for a pad and started scribbling furiously. After a brief period of activity, he looked up and turned the pad toward me. "See this?" he demanded. I answered that I did, and he began with some passion, "Here's what I'm responsible for. Do you see communication anywhere on that list?" I had to agree that I didn't.

He went on, "Look, I'm as good as my last thirty days. If my last thirty days are good, I'm a hero. If not, I'm a bum. It's as simple as that. So thanks but no thanks. I don't have time to do what I think you want me to.

"Further, let me tell you a story. Last month, I pulled the sales team in for an all-day meeting to see what some of our issues were and how we could better address them. We missed our targets for the month, and I got reprimanded for pulling them off the street. So not only do you not get rewarded for communication, you get punished.

"But let me tell you something else," he went on. "I'm a smart guy, and I know that if you communicate effectively you get results. And if you don't, you don't. So I promise you that if I ever get the time and support, I'll talk to those people and listen to them, but for now it's not going to happen. End of interview."

He spoke for thousands if not millions of his fellow managers and supervisors in all kinds of companies, then and now. At first I was distressed, but as I reflected on the experience I realized that there was a flaw in his pragmatic reasoning. He clearly saw communication with his reports as an extracurricular activity to be attended to when all of the other responsibilities were taken care of. It's not extracurricular. It's integral to the entire task of managing people. The question was how to show that convincingly and to put the necessary supporting tools around it.

What resulted initially was a model that I developed over time to demonstrate the six questions that are inherent in every manager-employee relationship in any work setting (although they don't necessarily occur in the nice, neat order in which I'm showing them). Here are the first three:

- *What's my job?* In brief, what do you expect me to do around here? What are the boundaries of my job? What constitutes success, and what does failure look like?

- *How am I doing?* Is my performance meeting or exceeding expectations? Where might I not be measuring up? What do I need to work on?

- *Does anyone care?* Okay, I'm now a fully functioning employee, doing what's expected well, and more. Does anyone notice? Does the company care? Does anyone care about me?

Note that all three of these initial questions are intimately focused on "me and my needs." In a sense, fulfilling them is the price of admission into the head and the motivation of the person being supervised.

If these needs are indeed fulfilled, then I argue that the employee has what some may regard as a higher set of needs. At the point of fulfillment, it is natural for people to begin to look at causes larger than themselves. That's when they begin to think in terms of *us* rather than merely *me*. So the remaining three questions shift to *us*, as follows:

- *How are we doing?* The initial focus here is necessarily on the immediate work team because that's the closest group that the individual belongs to. At this point, he or she begins to care about the team's objectives and how well they are being met.

Once that's settled, the next question is more abstract; it has to do with company goals, direction, and vision:

- *What's our vision, mission, and values?* Here we get to the basic issue that people don't work for bread alone. They have a need to belong to something important, something bigger than themselves in which they can take pride and satisfaction. At this point they identify with the organization and want to see "a line of sight"—in other words, they want to understand how their role and work contributes to the larger cause. They also want to be part of an enterprise that is admired and respected. As a small indicator, think of all of the company paraphernalia, logos, and the like that people wear on their person as an outward sign that they belong to something worth belonging to.
- *How can I help?* I believe this last question is one that is earned by the company and the immediate manager. In effect, it is the gift of engagement offered willingly by a knowledgeable and committed employee who has been properly led and communicated with.

If you look closely at these six questions, you will see how well they track with all of the needs catalogued in the preceding chapter.* Figure 4.1 shows what the six questions look like, in the form of a model of employee communication needs. Notice how traditional this model really is in terms of what we say are the important leadership issues in organizations. It's little more than communicating the basics. Yet it's amazing how often these simple basics are overlooked in practice.

The one person best equipped to satisfy these needs is the frontline counterpart of the Xerox branch manager in New York who inspired the model. Frontline managers are the only ones

Figure 4.1: Understanding an Employee's Communication Needs on the Job.

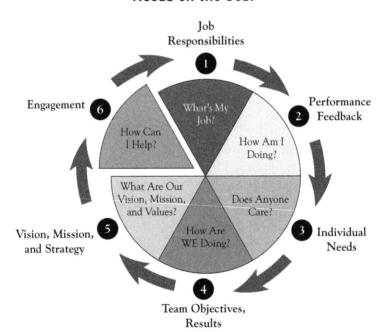

close enough to the action to satisfy all of these critical needs. But they won't do it, any more than the branch manager would, without permission, encouragement, inspection, and support. Most of the effort here has to be accomplished face-to-face. In the instance of the three "I" questions, it's a matter of one-on-one communication in which the manager plays the important role of mentor and coach.

For the three "we" questions, most of the effort is group communication, in which the manager makes sure the team understands its charter and goals and the ongoing results against those goals. That's a role much more akin to being a quasi cheerleader or a facilitator, making sure that the team meets often in productive sessions in which important team issues are discussed and hashed over.

The larger communication issues of vision, mission, values, and key organizational challenges are primarily the province of the senior leadership, who need to inspire and excite the members of the organization. For the professional communicator, supporting this role should be a familiar task. But here again the frontline managers have a key role to play. They are the interpreters. It falls to them to communicate what these larger messages mean to the work team and their responsibilities.

Given that in all of the research employees give slightly better marks to supervisors and other frontline managers on communication and trust issues than they do to senior management, this is a significant credibility opportunity. Organizations need to capitalize on the trust and high credibility that most frontline managers enjoy by supporting and encouraging their face-to-face communication efforts.

Making It All Work

To enable and support the manager in this important and fundamental communication role, senior leaders need to focus on four things—accountability, strategy, training, and tools.

The accountability issue is key. Everyone knows that what gets done in organizations is what is stated, inspected, and rewarded as a priority. That means the organization that wishes to capitalize on effective face-to-face communication makes it clear that such communication is a fundamental part of the manager's job.

There's no better way to do that than to ensure that every manager or supervisor is trained to understand the importance of this communication role. This is a matter of awareness training rather than skills training. Gathering a group of managers in a room and telling them that you're going to "teach them how to communicate" is a sure-fire formula to accomplish two things—failed training and offended, angry managers. My Xerox branch manager knew perfectly well how to communicate. He even knew how important it was. What he lacked was the awareness that communication was not an extracurricular activity to be attended to when there was time. No one can blame him for caving into senior management's pressure for results; what he could be blamed for was not fully understanding what it all meant to the effectiveness of the people he led, as well as to his own success. In a better world he and others like him would be encouraged and held accountable in fulfilling this communication role as the means to achieving the organization's ends.

In fact, that's what ultimately happened at Xerox as more and more leadership training was initiated. Much of the Leadership Through Quality initiative that Xerox eventually used to solve its serious competitive issues in the 1980s and 1990s—and to win the Baldridge quality award—was communication based.

Accountability implies inspection and measurement. This is a bit sticky, because the measures of communication effectiveness have not been very well defined or quantified up to this point. We need a model like the one I've shown that becomes the basis of awareness training. Once that's accomplished, the best judges of whether a given manager is effectively performing his or her communication role are the people who work for him. That can be gauged by using some sort of upward evaluation device. It's a relatively simple matter to create such surveys and to ensure that they are used to measure a given manager's communication effectiveness. In that way the accountability becomes real, and if the manager's performance review is based at least to some degree on communication effectiveness, the loop is closed.

To make that fair, the training and the necessary support tools must be in place. Those tools can range from simple talking points to meeting tips and tools to elaborate intranet portals where managers get the information they need to deliver to their people. And of course all of this must be driven by a coherent strategy that accounts for the whole process—accountability, awareness training, and support tools.

One further important factor here is the example of senior leaders. To the extent that they model the kind of communication behavior they require from their managers and supervisors, the whole thing takes on an importance and a reality that makes it work.

High Tech and High Touch

It's tempting, in an organization with a high saturation of technology, to rely on more and more remote communication by busy managers and supervisors. There is story after story of the manager who communicates primarily by email, even to the point of not walking a few steps to deliver a message personally. For the introverted or the merely busy and stressed, this is a handy out. The trouble with this, as we all know, is that such communication is absent tone of voice, body language, or context and thus easily open to misunderstanding and misinterpretation.

Globalization and even the distribution of workers in scattered locations make this problem even more difficult. So the conscientious manager needs to have a personal strategy to ensure that he or she is augmenting high tech with high touch. The study cited in Chapter Two on information movement showed that too much online communication leads to loneliness and a sense of alienation; these findings should be kept in mind by all those who manage people. As simple a technique as picking up the telephone and making contact with workers who are geographically dispersed is a help. Better yet, a fistful of airline tickets and the time spent to appear onsite in person does wonders for communication.

Senior leaders who doubt this should consider the following anecdote. In a focus group at a leading Silicon Valley company, one participant asked me drily, "Has anyone told you the difference between our CEO and Elvis?" The amused faces around the table showed that this was a common joke on the employee grapevine. "No," I admitted. Instantly, he deadpanned, "Elvis has been sighted."

Face-to-Face and the Professional Communicator

It's tempting, as I've said, for the professional communicator to presume that effective face-to-face communication is none of her business. Those who define their responsibility as being simply the keepers of employee media are especially prone to this view. The trouble is, employees rarely see such media, including the company intranet, as their primary communication sources in the company.

I often run focus groups in which I ask the participants to identify their primary internal and external communication sources for what is going on in the company, as well as company priorities. I map their replies, with the internal sources on the inside of a circle and the external sources on the outside. It's always instructive that the initial responses all have to do with things like meetings, teams on which they serve, their bosses, coworkers, and other live-and-in-person sources. After several minutes, they may or may not identify the various company media as sources, and when they do it's usually with a dismissive tone.

Credibility, it seems, has much to do with human presence. And face-to-face communication is its most valuable technique.

5

OPENNESS

A word that is common currency among communication professionals, organizational leaders, and employees is *openness*—that quality of institutional organizations that connotes their willingness to create an open communication climate in which information is widely shared. But determining when, where, and with whom to share that information is not a simple matter.

The Enron scandal that first reached public attention in 2001 and the dishonest manipulations of financial results by scores of other companies have led to a renewed public demand for transparency and access to company information. Although openness and transparency may at first blush seem to be the same thing, they are not. Openness implies the willingness of an institutional organization to make information widely available to its members, who have a legitimate and obvious need for that information. The open organization does its best to avoid unnecessary secrecy and elaborate justifications of who needs to know what. The assumption is that everyone in the company has a clear need to know as much as possible about company operations and plans without compromising proprietary or personal information. It is a matter of trusting one another to act in the best interests of the organization.

Transparency is perhaps the ultimate aspect of openness. It implies that all organizations must operate in such a way that any interested outside party can examine the organization's behavior and its records with minimal or no restrictions. Publicly traded organizations must respect this demand as a condition of their right to exist and must give equal access to all existing and potential investors.

Transparency is the logical demand of a society in which secrets are regarded as sinister and the likely result of misdeeds. In an age in which information is freely available and plentiful and cases like Enron have added to public outrage, it is not surprising that there is an expectation that secrecy implies wrongdoing. Yet because of the intense nature of competition and legitimate proprietary interests, organizations tend to resist outright transparency, which they see as a threat to their best interests. There is a fine line between respecting the public's right to know and not giving away the store.

In fact, real transparency in a highly competitive world can be downright dangerous. The risk, always, is that the competition will gain an advantage from knowing your competitive strategy or your plans to introduce this or that product or service. In a wired world in which corporate espionage is a recognized practice, it's hard to persuade any leadership that it's in their best interests to be open about their intentions or their vulnerabilities.

Publicly held companies are subject to all kinds of disclosure rules in regard to their financial dealings, so it's a balancing act for them to ensure that they operate within the law without revealing anything that will threaten their competitive advantage. Privately held companies face only their own tendencies to release or withhold information and their concerns about the consequences.

The dilemma in both cases, however, is the internal communication issue. How do you run a company without sharing sensitive information with the players who have to help you win the game? Particularly if information is a raw material, what do you do to share it with those who need it to do their jobs even as you protect it from getting into the wrong hands? There are no easy answers to that dilemma, but in the Information Age it's clear that too strong a tendency to protect information and withhold it from employees is self-defeating. It would be like keeping an athletic team in the dark about what it takes to win as well as the strategy for winning. Yet some companies treat their workforce in roughly that fashion when they are overly protective of information.

All of this makes life difficult for the communication professional, whose normal inclination is to want to share and distribute information. Indeed, as I stated earlier, through the years many of my colleagues have harbored a wish that they could function much like the public media. It's tempting to see parallels between the corporate communication task and the information services provided by the public media. Although reporters and other journalists often harbor a not-very-well-hidden disdain for so-called "corporate flacks," it is undeniable that the basic skills required of both groups are almost identical. They both interview, listen, process, observe, write, and publish in some fashion. In fact, the likelihood is that they were even college classmates.

But the similarities end there. Corporate communication professionals, regardless of their journalistic training and inclinations, are advocates. Objectivity, although important to their functioning, is not their highest priority. In my personal view that doesn't mean that they should be little more than hired guns, but let's not kid ourselves that they are hired to be objective, investigative reporters within their organizations. In fact, that would be a ludicrous role for any institutional leadership to sponsor.

That said, they must have enough integrity to respect the truth and the public's right to know information that affects the public welfare. That also goes for the employee's right to know as much information about the company as his or her well-being and sense of security require. In the final analysis, communication professionals must remain faithful and ethical advisors to their leadership. If they can't perform that role in good conscience for reasons of personal integrity or even reservations about the organization's leadership and its behavior, then I strongly believe they should go elsewhere where they can lead more authentic lives. Life is far too short to do otherwise.

What Employees Need to Know

On the issue of what information to share and what not to share, the standard is sometimes based on who needs to know what and when they need to know it. This notion of "need to know" is a tricky one. The term originated with the military and dealt with the need to protect military secrets. Its doctrine separates those with a need for certain kinds of information from those who have only a casual interest or, more to the point, from those with malicious motives who would compromise the information if they could—or even use it to the detriment of its owner. This doctrine in the military and in government leads to rigid categories of information sharing and restricts access to those with a demonstrable need for the information.

The need-to-know doctrine always holds sway in nations in times of war and national emergency, sometimes creating significant conflicts with constitutional rights and other rights and needs. I remember well the World War II veterans I worked under in my first communication positions, who were so influenced by their military experience that they would often invoke "need to know" to question the sharing of a given piece of information. Their inevitable question was whether people truly needed to know this or that bit of information or whether their need was only a matter of curiosity. It's a dangerous notion when applied broadly in an organization. Overly cautious leaders can easily hide behind it to withhold information that should be shared widely. And in government it can undermine precious personal rights of access to information the public has a right and need to know.

Cautious and secretive corporate leaders often believe that information sharing is inherently dangerous. So the ultimate question is, just what kind of information do employees really need to know? In today's world, in which knowledge workers perform much of the work and depend on the free flow of information, the answer is, as much information as possible without compromising proprietary information, confidential information about future competitive plans, or personal information about coworkers. Everything else should be fair game.

Are there risks in such a broad reading of people's need to know? The risks are far greater from not sharing vital information and leaving the workforce in the dark about matters of vital concern to them. The hard truth is that nimble competitors already know much of what the leadership may be trying to protect. Does it make sense then to keep the same information from the people who must execute the strategy and plans the leadership depends on? Clearly not.

It's maddening for employees when company leaders are willing to share confidential information with, say, security analysts or reporters, and then refuse to talk with employees about the same issues. Reading about one's future or current company plans in the *Wall Street Journal* or local papers when nothing has been said inside the organization is bound to anger employees every time it happens. In some few instances, because of federal securities regulations, it's necessary to reveal financial information in such a way that no one party benefits or suffers from it. In those cases, wise leaders ensure that employees are informed immediately after the release of such information. They also do the best they can to explain exactly why they are constrained and to tell employees as much as the law allows. Such announcements rarely cause much of a stir among employees when they are handled with that degree of openness.

As noted earlier, the most successful communication formula is a simple one. Again, it boils down to this: (1) where is this organization proposing or planning to go, (2) how does it propose to get there, and (3) what does all of that mean to me? If we keep that simple formulation in mind every time there is a discussion of what to communicate or not communicate to a workforce, we can't go too far wrong.

Those three questions, if taken as seriously as they should be, imply that the leadership of an organization will be forthcoming to employees about business or other strategies of concern and that they will make the important connection between the external circumstances that drive the behavior of an organization and the strategic steps the organization is taking to cope with those circumstances. Articulating those connections is absolutely critical, for the simple reason that they are not always obvious to those not directly involved in making strategic and tactical decisions for the organization.

Too often organizational leaders talk about strategy or future plans in isolation without discussing *why* they are taking the actions they propose to take. In fact, most companies and other organizations are pretty good at talking about the *what* of their actions and lousy at talking about the *why*. Without the explanation of why, it's inevitable that people will resort to speculation based on insufficient information. Most of the time that speculation is far from flattering about the leadership's real motives or intentions. There's just enough paranoia and suspicion in institutional organizations to fuel that suspicion, so leaders are well advised not only to offer a candid description of their plans and actions but also to make sure they explain and connect cause and effect and not leave that open to speculation.

Change Communication and Openness

Candid and detailed communication is especially helpful in times of significant change. The problem for the members of an organization in the face of change is that their comfortable perceptions of the reality of their work lives are shattered. Suddenly there is a new reality to deal with, along with the need to begin making the connections between necessity and response at both a personal and an organizational level.

As rational people, we expect rational behavior from the people who lead us. When that rational behavior is seemingly absent, we become more and more unsettled by the change. This situation can be avoided by explaining change in terms of the circumstances or forces that make the proposed strategy or action a rational response to those forces. That's especially true when trying to explain strategic initiatives in terms that make sense to those who must carry them out. (More about that in Chapter Seven on the marketplace and its influence on communication essentials.)

Obviously, the most important of the three questions of direction, planning, and meaning is the third: what does it all mean to *me*? In the throes of any change that an individual would regard as important or threatening, that's the ultimate question. How is this going to affect my life? Is it a threat? Is it a potential gain? How should I regard it, finally?

Everyone who has ever worked for any company or large institutional organization is familiar with the circumstance of hearing an important announcement and then having to wait weeks or months for the announced action to play out. The most excruciating situation is that of the organization that has announced that it must take drastic action to deal with its current business results and then unfolds those actions for the next several weeks and months without informing people, during that period of uncertainty, of their respective fates.

Most so-called downsizings follow that familiar pattern. There's trouble in River City, and here's its nature and some of our options. Stay tuned; we'll let you know our plans as they unfold. In the meantime the workforce loses both its motivation and its productivity as people focus on the unknown dangers that face them personally. Inevitably, during this period the high-performing individuals with other options decide to end the uncertainty and pursue those options. The result is the loss of the very people the organization can least afford to lose.

Too often, the dilemma for the leadership is that they are dealing with all sorts of possible scenarios and don't have hard answers to the questions individuals want answered. In my view the simplest strategy to deal with this dilemma is to empower managers and supervisors to quietly inform those at risk and to reassure those who are not. That may seem like a dangerous communication strategy, but it beats the extended anxiety that otherwise grips the workforce and destroys performance in times of prolonged uncertainty.

More to the point, it is fairer to those who are most vulnerable in the wake of significant change. Companies and other organizations usually weather such change; individuals, with their obligations and responsibilities to family and career, often don't. And the survivors get either a positive or negative primary lesson in the values and behavior of the organization and its leaders that employ them—a lesson that tends to color their views for years to come.

Examples of Openness

Jack Stack, the founder and CEO of SRC Holding Corporation, is the leading advocate of the leadership style that has come to be known as Open-Book Management. SRC is an often-cited and classic example of open leadership, a company that has managed to run its operations on the basis of completely open communication. By opening the books to its employees, keeping them informed of results in real time, and permitting them to share in company profits through innovative employee bonus arrangements, the company has achieved an impressive record of success that continues at the time of this writing.

Stack concluded long ago that secrecy—keeping the workforce in the dark—was an important cause of business failure. In most companies there has been traditionally what he calls *three levels of ignorance*. The first level is top management's presumption that the workforce is incapable of understanding the leadership's problems and responsibilities in the same way the leaders do. At the second level, he says, are people who are ignorant of why senior leaders are doing what they're doing, so they chalk up every company miscue to a mixture of greed and stupidity.

At the third level of ignorance, according to Stack, middle managers and supervisors are kept in the dark about the why of actions and motives, so they are constantly torn between the demands of senior management and the needs of the workforce. If they side with one, they anger the other. This leaves them in constant turmoil, making theirs one of the most difficult positions in most companies.

This third level of ignorance and keeping people in the dark about the why of actions and motives is especially pernicious. Effective supervisors and frontline managers of all kinds are the ones who must be able to translate company strategy and tactics to the level of the people for whose work they are responsible. People tend to identify with those circumstances closest to their day-to-day experience, so a supervisor who can provide the context for that experience is an invaluable member of the work team. As noted in the previous chapter, that requires training, accountability, tools, and information. And not incidentally, in an age in which more and more communication is delivered through technology, it provides high touch in a high-tech era.

In my own career, one such natural-born leader and the coleaders with whom she's surrounded herself provide hope for the future of open leadership. I first met Barbara Fagan-Smith, the founder of a Silicon Valley–based communication consultancy, when she invited me to become a member of the advisory board she had set up to counsel her fledging firm, ROI Communication.

Fagan-Smith and her original leadership team, consisting of Barbara Baill and Sheryl Lewis, had left executive positions at Quantum Corporation in 2001. Intelligent and accomplished young women with family responsibilities, they were determined to start their own company specializing in internal communication consulting. As mothers with busy lives and active children, they decided from the start that they would create a firm that was sympathetic not only to the needs of young and middle-aged career women but also to the needs of their clients and consultants generally. That meant being family-friendly and even having the courage to put their values where their money was. The payoff in 2007 was that ROI Communication was named by *Working Mother* magazine as one of the nation's twenty-five best small companies for its "creative family-friendly programs."

Much of the success of ROI is attributable to the leadership's resolve to operate not only a family-friendly company but also one that is completely open to its staff. Fagan-Smith and her leadership team run frequent WebEx sessions in which its consultants, most of whom work out of home offices when they are not at client locations, can be updated about company results, challenges, and actions and recognized for their contributions. Every January a one-day company meeting gathers the entire sixty-person staff in a face-to-face dialogue to look at the year ahead.

ROI consultants even get to collectively update the company strategy and make recommendations for the year's upcoming strategic priorities, based on their intimate knowledge of client needs. Those recommendations are then collected and communicated to the staff to determine which ones elicit the greatest consensus. The leadership team adds their goals, and the final agreed-on priorities then become the focus of the business for that year or for whatever time it takes to achieve them. It is participation to the max, based on complete information sharing. Company results speak for themselves, as the company's revenue and client base have grown more than threefold in its six-year history.

An important question is whether large companies can operate in this open fashion or if this is possible only in a small company in which hierarchy and authority don't make much sense in the first place. One answer comes from the example of a large and complex state agency charged with the administration of the health care benefits and pensions of that state's employees. At this agency, secrecy and political infighting were once commonplace. Agency employees worked mostly in the dark about agency issues and problems. They were regarded as pension experts and paper shufflers who were simply expected to do their backroom jobs.

A newly appointed leader, whom we'll refer to as Ed, was a charismatic and informal person determined to change all of this. Working with an employee committee, he initiated a study of the information people were lacking and that they needed to better understand the agency's workings. He was committed and successful in a hands-on effort to initiate the changes that were necessary to end the agency's long tradition of secrecy and a general lack of openness in the employee climate. He was especially effective in recognizing employee accomplishments and nurturing a climate of personal leadership. As a result, his administration was wildly successful, steering the agency through a time of efficiency, productivity, and success in which his leadership was widely recognized as exceptional in its openness and efficiency.

But after a few years of making the agency one of the most progressive in his state, Ed decided that it was time to move on. In the aftermath of his leaving, the agency was hit with what his remaining staff called a perfect storm of events. Rising health care costs threatened the agency's operations. Pension reform was a serious topic of conversation, with a growing debate on the practice of defined benefits (a guaranteed pension after so many years of service) versus the relatively new notion of defined contribution plans (employee cash investments over the years in 401[k] type plans that would yield a benefit based on those contributions). The state's politicians, worried about current and future debt and the coming retirement of the baby boom generation, leaned toward the defined contribution solution.

Even without those challenges, the agency still was facing changing workforce demographics and a changing view of what retirement was becoming in today's aging society. On top of all of this, the political climate was anything but friendly. All of those conditions were forcing the agency leadership to think more analytically and strategically and to become a more nimble, focused organization.

It was a time when employees truly needed an appreciation of the events that were overtaking the agency. It was also, however, a time of transition to a new leader and a different management philosophy. Peter, who took over from Ed, was not by nature an open communicator. Worse, he was beset with all of the change and political turmoil that were coming his way and preoccupying his time and energy. Little attention was paid to the need to include the workforce in what was going on.

At the same time, it was clear that the agency had to undergo important change, from an organization with a culture focused on efficient completion of its transactions with state employees to one more focused on analysis and strategic change. It also had to change from a culture of slow, deliberate decision making to fast (yet still deliberate) decision making. Most important, in the view of the new leadership, the agency workforce had to give up its complacency and become more aware of the changing marketplace that was requiring all this significant operational change.

Agency research showed that employees again felt they were being kept in the dark by the new regime. As a result, they had begun to believe that some sort of secret plan was being concocted by the leadership to make dramatic changes in the agency and the way it operated. They were also convinced that the leaders did not respect their needs in this time of turmoil. Thus they felt powerless, overworked, and ill-informed. The absence of any solid information seemed to generate one of two employee reactions—fear for the future or a denial of the facts and continued complacency.

Once Peter fully understood the extent of the employee reaction and what it was doing to the need to enlist employee support in change, he undertook a major initiative to inform agency employees of the facts they were collectively facing. He became as hands-on as Ed had been and determined to work for greater employee understanding and support.

The agency slowly but surely regained its reputation for openness and for candid communication with its people, a tradition it continues to work hard to maintain. The problems have not gone away, but the staff willingness to deal with those problems and to accept the necessary changes has increased dramatically.

A Case of Inevitability

In still another argument for greater openness in organizations, the technologists loudly proclaim that there is no alternative; that today's robust technology—so common in practically every organization—doesn't just facilitate information sharing, but actually makes it impossible not to share. Couple that, they say, with a generation that has grown up with Google and Yahoo! and the expectation of freely available information, and you're kidding yourself if you think that there's a choice. Or that any organization can maintain a climate of secrecy with its workforce even if it wished to.

Given the need to defuse the suspicions and fears of a skeptical workforce, greater openness could also prove to be a powerful antidote to that skepticism. In the Information Age, everyone in the organization has a need to know.

6

RESEARCH

Organizational leaders tend to be conservative souls. How often have you heard one of them espouse that famous bit of folk wisdom, "If it ain't broke, don't fix it?" My response to that homely bromide has always been, "How would you like to fly on an airline that lived by that slogan? 'Take Your Chances Airline—if it ain't broke, don't fix it.'"

Yet many CEOs and their colleagues would prefer to live by that simplistic slogan when it comes to communicating bad news or even to determining the proper role of the communication team. Some even have the quaint notion that the less said to employees about the business or leadership intentions, the better. Those are the folks who think internal communication should be mostly about service anniversaries, photos of the Christmas party in January, and a few grip-and-grin shots of the boss shaking hands with the latest person he or she wants to recognize.

What's needed is to show them what former Honeywell CEO Larry Bossidy used to call the "burning platform." His metaphor had to do with the story of a fire on an oil rig in the ocean and the dilemma faced by the oil workers on board. Do they stay and face certain death or do they make the terrifying leap into the freezing waters of the North Sea in the hope of saving their lives?

His view was that organizations facing traumatic change confront pretty much the same philosophical question. Once you acknowledge the fact that your organization is facing serious change, do you simply hang on and hope for the best or does the figurative burning platform become the motivation to jump into the unknown? In the Xerox case with which I began this book, the initial choice seemed to be to hang around until the flames became so hot that there was no choice. *Throw a few hands overboard, but let the rest of us huddle together away from the smoke and flames and see what happens.*

Data Gathering

About the only way that I know of to persuade reluctant senior leaders to face the music of change and dance is to gather the data that show just how serious things are. Times of stress and change offer perfect opportunities to look at communication strategy as well as to consider the proper mission of the communication function and its potential reinvention. Uninformed workers are often distracted and unproductive workers as they struggle to understand the organization's directions and plans and their own unique role going forward.

Even in the absence of any dramatic and compelling evidence supporting the need for change, it is still important and instructive to research your audience's communication needs. Those needs, like the needs of any consumer of information, should be the starting point for all communication strategy. The standing research, cited in Chapter Three on employee information needs, provides a solid frame for all of those efforts. But it's important to fill in the details of the picture in your own organization, because there are inevitable differences from organization to organization—even in the same company.

If you agree with the commonsense proposition that the information needs of the audience should be the starting point for all employee communication strategy, then how do you gather the information you need to justify change and to design that strategy? Some would argue that this is not a do-it-yourself project; that to do the job right you need an outside, objective source that is more likely to be credible to your leadership. I'd be the last one to discourage the use of real experts. My own view is, that's the best way to go if you can afford it and providing you find the right outside counsel. If you don't have the budget, I recommend that you put aside your misgivings and take a crack at doing your own research. It beats guessing, in any case. Here are some tips on how to proceed. (By the way, if you do have the budget for valuable outside counsel, I would still argue that these are the issues they should be exploring with your participation and collaboration.)

Most consultants insist on fact gathering before they offer any counsel. It's a bit like going to a doctor for a checkup during which he or she generally will listen to your list of complaints, make some educated observations about the symptoms you present, and then order tests to verify those first impressions. The model shown in Figure 6.1 is a bit like a checkup for an organization's communication process. It is a tried and tested consulting model that follows the numbered path shown.

The Executive Interviews

The organization assessment (sometimes known as a communication audit) depicted here typically begins with a series of one-on-one interviews with key members of the executive staff. The objective of these interviews is to get a firsthand sense of

Figure 6.1: Map of an Organization Assessment.

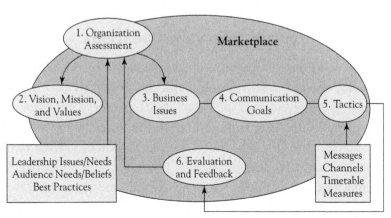

the issues that they see as paramount to the organization's success. In each of these interviews, which typically should take about an hour, you are trying to get an individual and ultimately a collective look at the organization's strengths and vulnerabilities. In the interviews you also will get a firsthand look at the vision and values of the organization as espoused by the senior leadership as well as their own sense of the communication priorities the organization faces.

If you are a good listener and a patient interviewer, you will get an unprecedented view of your organization in all its glory—and even its ugliness. After a half dozen or so of these interviews, you will find that a story is unfolding. Generally it will be a consistent story, but sometimes there are important variations on the theme. At the end of the effort you will have an excellent understanding of the issues your organization faces, both short and long term, as well as the degree of leadership consensus on those issues. Interestingly, there is not always consensus—a fact that's valuable for both them and you to understand.

Sometimes these interviews are also augmented by a series of additional interviews with selected people "in the know." These are generally people in key positions with a particular outlook or grasp of the situation. Such a list can often be surfaced by a simple question: is there anyone else not on my list that you would particularly like me to interview as part of this process?

Typical Interview Questions

The following list of possible interview questions is offered only to suggest the issues you should explore. Obviously you need to develop the right set of tailored questions for your situation. Notice especially in Figure 6.1 that the assessment model is embedded in the space labeled "the marketplace." That's deliberate, because the marketplace is the pervasive influencer of an organization's strategy. So the initial questions you need answered are all focused on the marketplace and its impact on strategy. (More about that marketplace impact in the next chapter.) These represent a typical, generic list of questions for the interviews:

- What market forces (such as customer needs, competitive initiatives, opportunities, and so forth) are driving our organization's strategy?
- Briefly, what is that strategy? How are we responding to the marketplace?
- What are the main obstacles to success in implementing our strategy?
- What is your vision for the business? What are the opportunities that excite you as you look at our potential?
- What values guide our behavior in running the business? Particularly, what values guide our leadership and our treatment of the people who make up the workforce?
- What do you see as the critical success factors for the business? What do these factors say about what our priorities should be?
- What does success look like for us? What are the vital measures that tell us whether we are winning or losing?
- As you look into the future, what worries you most? What are the company's vulnerabilities?
- What do you want employees to understand better about the company and their jobs?

Inevitably, these questions lead to other related issues that you may well want to explore in the interview. It is not that unusual that one question may be so provocative and the answers so interesting that they overtake the interview and render the other questions moot. Remember that you're not just conducting an interview; you are searching for the kind of information that can help shape the content of company communications for both the short- and long-term future. In that regard it is often useful to send your list of questions to the interviewees in advance to help improve the quality of their responses.

Focus Groups

Once the interviews are completed, my favorite next step usually is a series of focus group discussions with employees at various levels of the organization. This is your opportunity to listen to the people in the trenches—to hear their insights, prejudices, and often-skeptical views of the leadership and their initiatives. Running such focus groups calls for intense listening to both what is said and what is implied. It also calls for the skill of gentle prodding to get behind sometimes-cryptic statements. But done well it is a fascinating counterpoint and expansion of the story that is unfolding before you. I often compare the experience of an organization assessment with reading a mystery novel in which the heroes, villains, and victims quickly reveal themselves. What is called for here on your part is absolutely nondefensive, neutral listening.

Guidelines for Focus Groups

I believe that focus groups are one of the richest possible means of gathering employee opinions and concerns. They permit you, as the facilitator, to probe, observe body language and levels of passion or disinterest, and maneuver the conversation to get at people's real perceptions of the communication process as *they* experience it. Keep in mind there is a good chance that your views of that process are very different from the views of the people who make up the focus group. Avoid the temptation to narrow the discussion to their perceptions of *your* ongoing communication efforts. What they think of the company intranet or the CEO's blog is far less significant than their view of the overall communication process as they experience it daily.

The key to successful focus groups is neutral, nondefensive, and sympathetic listening that quickly builds the trust levels you need to coax out people's honest views. Experience shows that what the participants regard as "communication" typically involves all of the information and situations they experience in trying to do their jobs to the best of their ability. Because of the status and authority levels built into organizations, the perspectives at various levels are likely to differ and sometimes even contradict one another. Middle managers and supervisors, for example, often see things differently from workers in a call center or in a sales office. The point is that people's honest perceptions of the communication experience and of the organization and its leadership are really what you're after.

Here are some focus group procedural guidelines based on long experience:

- The best size for such a group is twelve to fifteen participants, a range that offers an opportunity for dialogue and nondefensive probing for understanding, in which any reluctant participants are likely to find a degree of safety.

- The selection should be random based on a computer run, but it's essential that the participants in a given group should all be at the same official level in the organization. For example, there should be no supervisors in a group of manufacturing or service workers and no professionals the group would find threatening, and conversely, no "lower-level" workers in a group of supervisors. It is also advisable to have participants from different parts of the organization so that you don't get bogged down in parochial issues.

- In general, executive assistants should be ineligible to participate. They are too closely identified with their bosses and often are seen, fairly or unfairly, as company spies who will report the conversation back to their bosses.

- If you have a union in your organization, it is advisable to communicate to the union's leadership that the focus groups will be held to gather employee views about company communication practices. They may object, but they have no authority to block their members from participating.

- Participants should be invited personally by memo or email, with the opportunity to decline if they so prefer. It makes sense to issue the invitation over the signature of a senior leader to give the process credibility and official sanction. There should be no rewards for participating, as they tend to bias the group by potentially attracting otherwise uninterested participants.

- Sessions should be held in a comfortable conference room with small amenities such as coffee, cookies, and the like to help relax the group.

- The optimum length of time for a focus group is ninety minutes, so the group has time enough to judge whether they trust you and what information they want to pass along.

- It is generally better for two people to lead the group, one to facilitate and the other to take notes. Also, two people are better able to take in the group's intentions and messages and later compare notes on what they heard.

- It is helpful to have the note taker use a flip chart visible to all as he or she captures the relevant points. This open approach promotes trust and gives the group the opportunity to correct misunderstandings.

- In the beginning of the session you need to introduce yourself by name, tell the group the purpose of the discussion, and assure them that the exercise is anonymous and that there will be no attribution of any comments either to individuals or to the focus group as a whole. This approach is important to establish the kind of trust and candor necessary for a successful dialogue. It is also important to avoid nametags, tent cards, or any other means of subverting or raising anxiety about anonymity.

- In facilitating, you need to keep the speech making by members to a minimum so that they don't dominate the discussion. If necessary, you can help shut that down by stating candidly that you need to hear the perspective of the entire group, not just a few individuals.

- It is not advisable to force people to participate with such tactics as "What's your opinion, Mary? You've been very quiet." Better to let Mary maintain her silence, even though its meaning is impossible to ascertain.

- The number of focus groups you organize depends on where you believe you may hear different messages or different perspectives from different locations. You need enough groups to show a decent representation but not so many that you are wasting your time listening to the same set of concerns over and over. In truth, most consultants will tell you that they pretty much have the pulse of the organization as well as the main story line after a half dozen or so of such groups, but you have to gauge what kind of numbers will provide you with a story that is credible to your leadership.

- In a small company it may be that you run many fewer groups or that you resort instead to individual anonymous interviews, with no attribution of comments, of course. The important thing is the message, not who sends it.

As noted, these are guidelines based on experience. You may think of other issues peculiar to your own company that dictate one modification or another.

The Focus Group Agenda

Again, what information you seek in the focus group is dependent on your own circumstances and objectives, but in general here is what you're looking for:

- Where do people go to get trustworthy information about the company and their jobs? Why are those the trusted sources? (Tip: It's helpful to make a flip chart list and tape it to the wall as a reminder for the rest of the session.)

- Once you have that list of communication sources, it's useful to ask which ones are the strengths (that is, the ones that best help them to understand the company and do their jobs more effectively). (Tip: Again, taping the page of responses to the wall is a helpful reminder and can be continued throughout the session.)

- Similarly, which ones are the least useful, the weakest (for example, not trustworthy, inaccurate, untimely, overly censored)?

- Next, can they say what is missing from their communication experience? In other words, what do they want to know that they don't know now? And where and from whom do they want to hear it?

- What, in their view and experience, is the impact of this missing or ineffective communication on their ability to perform their work properly?

- Finally, what suggestions do they have for action items that could address some of the needs they've surfaced?

In facilitating the session you will want to probe cryptic answers—the one-liners and phrases that are often loaded with implication but not immediately clear to the uninformed outsider.

What you will get from this exercise is lots of raw information and clues for the strategic recommendations you will finally make or for reinventing the communication process in your organization. Your task is to process it all as objectively as you can, make sense of what is doable and realistic, and then convert it to action recommendations you can defend.

What you have in hand, at the end, is *invaluable customer research* on the needs of your organization's various employee audiences. Use it wisely and honestly.

Best Practices

A parallel part of the effort is the gathering of best practices from those organizations you and your leadership admire. That should always be an ongoing process, but you can certainly launch a best practices study by contacting your counterparts in those organizations and interviewing them on what is working there and why. There is one caveat: you must understand that best practices often are so culturally based that they may or may not be transferable to a different kind of corporate culture.

Once you have gathered all of the information from the interviews, focus groups, and the best-practices study, the moment of truth is to sit down and interpret it all in a process that is generally more art than science. It is advisable to include at least two or three communication staff members in the assessment process so that you have the opportunity to compare impressions, challenge one another's views, and come to consistent conclusions. At this point you can begin to develop a set of communication objectives based on all that you have learned.

Here you are beginning to set the communication agenda for some time to come. Some of the possible key questions are

- What are the market influences that are shaping our business strategy?
- How does that strategy match up with and against those influences? Can we make the important case that the strategy is logically aligned to deal with the market influences?

- What does our senior leadership need to communicate to our workforce to enhance their credibility and persuade people that our strategy is rational and based on marketplace realities?

- What role does senior management need to play in all of this? What about ordinary line managers and their role?

- What is our proper role as a communication staff in helping people understand the big picture and our plan for winning in the marketplace?

- Do we need to be structured differently as a staff based on what we've heard? If so, what kind of organization makes the most sense? (Remember that structure always follows strategy and should be guided by the needs of the strategy.)

Other Company Research

In many instances, especially in large companies or organizations, there is other existing employee or customer research that has been done for one reason or another. In addition to the general types of data reported on employee needs in Chapter Three, this information can often be useful in supporting or corroborating your own findings. Seek out those other research efforts as an additional resource. The more validating data you have, the more persuasive your case.

Presenting Your Findings

After you have done as thorough an analysis of your findings as you possibly can, the next step is to determine the best way to present them along with a set of recommendations to your leadership. Most experienced consultants are careful to avoid the trap of surprising their senior clients with a shocking set of negative findings that are likely to be rejected out of hand. Instead, they tend to "socialize" their work at various stages of the effort, informing key participants of what they are beginning to hear and what they believe it means. Here is an art that no one can teach you. It is the simple, but important, process of avoiding a potential negative surprise that results in leadership denial and rejection of your findings as a result of that denial.

Be wary of scheduling an executive briefing before you have done the proper preparation of the senior leadership team. You do not want to be challenged and embarrassed by a doubting senior leader who has been surprised, embarrassed, or simply caught off guard by your findings or recommendations.

Another important technique is to make it clear that what you are reporting is *what you have heard* from the workforce. Emphasize that it is not your offhand opinion; it is the prevailing view of those you have listened to, whether or not you agree or disagree. Otherwise, you run the risk of being the messenger that needs to be punished for his or her delivery of bad news.

The news, incidentally, is not always bad. In fact, the good news always is how strongly people care and how much they want to see the organization do the right thing and succeed for the benefit of all concerned. A wise strategy in your report is to highlight the good news and the positive findings along with the negatives so that there is some degree of balance in what you are reporting.

Developing the Plan

The final part of the organization assessment is the normal translation of the objectives into tactics. Here is where you identify the messages, the most effective communication channels or new initiatives suggested by your research, and the timelines and the measures you will undertake to see if your objectives are being met. When you have completed that effort, you should present your recommendations to the appropriate levels of management to apprise them of how you believe your efforts need to be realigned or possibly how the mission of your staff may need to be reinvented consistent with the needs you've uncovered.

Unfortunately, no one can tell you exactly how to carry on this process in your own organization. So much of it depends on the level of support you normally enjoy, the willingness of your leaders to listen to new approaches, and your own skill in collaborating with natural allies in your organization to achieve the critical mass that generally is necessary to success. In that regard it's also important to keep your staff peers advised and included so that the not-invented-here phenomenon doesn't rear its ugly head. Remember that those who share responsibility can often be defensive and unsupportive if they haven't had a role in the research. In any of these efforts, collaboration and inclusion constitute the wisest policy.

In general, you will need to be patient, intelligent in picking your opportunities, and careful not to exceed people's capacity for change. You also need to be willing to go back to the drawing board when necessary. These things are always a work in progress, so compromise, flexibility, and the willingness to experiment—to carry on pilot projects and measure their success—are inevitably a part of the process. Realistic expectations all around also are important.

What you have in hand at the end is *invaluable customer research* on the needs of your organization's various employee audiences. Use it wisely and honestly in forming your communication strategy.

Quantitative Versus Qualitative Research

The organization assessment I recommend here is of the qualitative variety, which means that it is by definition less objective and somewhat more susceptible to human bias. How much more is questionable, as even the most objective survey suffers to some degree from such a bias. I recommend the qualitative approach if you are going to do this on your own; it is more consistent with the typical professional's skills in interviewing, probing, synthesizing, and reporting.

Quantitative research in the form of written surveys and the like is really the province of the survey expert rather than the educated amateur. For that reason I would not recommend homemade questionnaires unless you really know what you're doing. Writing survey questions that are as free as possible from bias and that truly seek the information you believe you're seeking—not to mention appropriate data analysis—is not a task for amateurs.

Furthermore, in my experience, if qualitative, anecdotal information from interviews and focus groups has face validity (that is, it rings true with the experience of most people in the organization and it matches leadership suspicions), it is generally accepted and not subject to any more challenge than are quantitative surveys. Although the results of such surveys are sometimes more persuasive to those who live and die by the numbers, they often suffer the disadvantage of being disruptive to the organization, create survey fatigue among the employee population, and are open to conflicting interpretations.

The other glaring disadvantage of surveys is the mystique of statistics itself, with its language of medians, midpoints, means, standard deviations, regression analyses, correlations, and other not-very-well-understood concepts among corporate leaders not versed in statistics. Good old-fashioned storytelling tends to have a lot more face value and impact than a presentation heavily laced with statistical calculations and comparisons that tend to confuse and distract from the import of the overall message you need to deliver. This claim will probably bring down the wrath of the statisticians and survey experts, but I've seen far too many senior leaders confused and irritated by complex data they couldn't readily comprehend or draw clear conclusions from. Once that happens, the blood is in the water, and the sharks begin circling.

Give me a good old-fashioned presentation every time with a simple story that includes a beginning, a middle, some solid observations, and a few well-chosen conclusions and recommendations.

Communication Measurement

A perennial research issue that occupies lots of time and discussion in the communication profession is the measurement of results. This subject has been recognized now for some years as critical to proving the contribution of effective communication to business success. It took on that kind of importance in the middle of the cost-cutting sprees that companies went on in the 1980s and '90s and beyond, when every function was asked to demonstrate its worth in measurable terms.

The challenge has been a difficult one. Aside from the fact that most practitioners were liberal arts and journalism majors deficient in statistics and other measurement skills, there was the obvious problem of proving the worth of such a subjective issue as communication. How were we to evaluate our contribution objectively?

The Holy Grail in this profession for as long as I can remember has been the wish to prove that a given communication initiative yielded X amount of bottom-line revenue or profit. That truly is the dream of fools or charlatans. Business results and success or failure are always the product of a complex cause-and-effect relationship that no one truly understands. If it were that easy, we would have long ago reduced all of this to simple formulas for business success.

The best we seem to be able to hope for is a *correlation* that demonstrates that communication is an important part of a complex set of causes. We argue, for example, that we have redoubled our communication efforts in a variety of ways, and revenue and profit have risen by X percent. Therefore, we can claim that our efforts correlate with that outcome. We can also compare ourselves with other companies that have marginal communication efforts and assert that their business results reflect a lack of attention to solid communication practice.

If you look at most of the studies that purport to demonstrate communication's value to the enterprise, you will usually find that kind of logic chain. How convincing is it to leaders who live and die by the numbers? I suspect their reactions range from dubious acceptance to outright skepticism.

Stu Reed, a senior executive at Motorola who has been recognized for his communication leadership as an operations executive, is philosophical about this issue. He calls it a "binary proposition." He says either you believe in the power of communication or you dismiss it as a soft endeavor that may or may not make a difference. That explanation works for him. It may well not for the numbers-minded people who lead so many companies.

The question of what and how to measure has tended to preoccupy the discussions of communication measurement. At ROI Communication we sponsor what we call the ROI Executive Communication Forum. It is an invitation-only group of communication executives at Fortune 200 companies or their equivalent. When we first gathered them together and asked what subjects they wanted to investigate as leading-edge issues, they quickly and unanimously chose metrics and the need to prove the value of their contributions to their companies.

In their initial conversations about what constitutes a state-of-the-art communication process at any company or organization, they identified the following six elements:

- The degree of employee engagement at that organization
- The value of the communication programs offered to employees
- The extent to which the communication content is aligned with and supportive of business goals
- The effectiveness of leader and line manager communication
- The degree to which communication promotes cross collaboration in the organization
- The extent to which communication affects employee behavior

This was also their collective conception of what should be measured in evaluating the effectiveness of any company communication process. It looks like a pretty solid starting point from which practitioners can continue to wrestle with this intriguing question of what and how to measure, together with determining what contribution effective communication strategy actually makes to business success. That there is an important connection is beyond dispute. What remains to be shown is the exact nature of that connection and how to manage it in such a way as to gain maximum return.

7

MARKETPLACE

When I led communication workshops in the early '90s, I often began somewhat facetiously by asking the group to raise their hands if their companies were in the throes of significant change. Inevitably, every hand in the room shot up. That decade wasn't exactly the beginning of the impact of intense global competition, but the competition was clearly being felt in spades by that time. The dot-com boom was in full flower, and the rest of the U.S. economy—largely because of the growing competition from Europe, Asia, India, and Latin America—was experiencing significant change.

That change of the early '90s was accelerated by a flurry of other important changes, including the subsequent and instructive dot-com bust, as well as the continuing export of much of our manufacturing capacity offshore to lower-wage countries, outsourcing of jobs to both domestic and international contractors, severe cost cutting leading to major downsizings in company after company, once solid and apparently ethical companies resorting to shady accounting practices to mask results, innovative technology that changed at a dizzying rate which led to increasing technical product obsolescence, and the end of once-dominant retail empires felled by cost-cutting competitors and fickle customers. The revolution was in full swing.

New York Times columnist Thomas Friedman characterizes the fundamental causes of this turbulent global change as "the triple convergence."[9] The first convergence and cause of the ongoing and chaotic change we're continuing to experience was the creation of a web-enabled playing field that allows for the sharing of knowledge, work, and collaboration on a global scale in real time.

That first convergence led to a second—the increasing ability of the collaborators to work together comfortably on a horizontal playing field and to create entirely new ways of doing business. So, for example, the supply-chain concept quickly evolved, in which one company collaborates horizontally with a variety of global suppliers, distributors, and installers to deliver an innovative new product that the originating company merely "organizes" for the customer. As a result, a Dell call center rep can query your particular needs, take an order, and sell you a computer customized to those needs. The actual computer then is manufactured, assembled, and packaged in China and delivered within days to your home by an overnight delivery service, all as a result of a series of well-timed handoffs.

The third convergence was the liberation of three billion people who had been frozen out of the global economy because they lived in formerly closed economies in Eastern Europe, Russia, China, India, other Asian countries, and Latin America. When these economies opened up, three billion people were freed to participate in the global economy and contribute their considerable talents and skills.

From Vertical to Horizontal Line of Sight

In the aftershock of the change that is being wrought by all of this, critical questions arise: How are people who have been accustomed to working and competing domestically in a vertical, hierarchical, authority-laden organization going to understand and deal with this radical new horizontal, global marketplace? What will it mean for their lives at work? And how are they going to adjust to the demands that are imposed on those lives?

I believe that the best answer to this dilemma is to expand their *line of sight*. This phrase applies to the need of the worker to understand how his or her contribution contributes to the enterprise. In the old industrial economy little thought was given to the widget makers' need to comprehend how, where, and when the part they manufactured fit into the final product. Even today studies show that only about one in five workers has a clear line of sight regarding his or her contribution.

I still have a clear visual recollection of rows of assembly line workers sitting at long benches assembling tiny electronic parts. It was at GE's Light Military Electronics Department, where I was then employed as a proposal and publicity writer. This facility was GE's design and manufacturing center for military and space guidance systems. The workers had no idea how their parts were used to guide a Polaris missile to its target or how their work enabled an Atlas guidance system to lift a satellite into orbit, nor did anyone think that it was important for them to know. They simply did their jobs as the prints directed, with little no attempt by anybody to satisfy their curiosity about end uses. They were only a part of an anonymous and, to them, amorphous system.

Likewise, much later, when I was consulting at a number of General Motors divisions, foreign competition was beginning to make serious inroads into the American car market. I well remember the consternation of the labor force over the complaints about American automobile quality. When told that there were quality issues with their products, the workers were perplexed and angry. "What do you mean, quality problems? I do quality work!" was their indignant reaction. Lacking a line of sight to the dealers and the customer, they could focus only on the task that had occupied them and that they performed to the best of their ability and to prevailing quality standards.

At a high-tech organization in Silicon Valley, groups of very savvy design engineers confessed that they didn't have a clue as to what their companies were facing as the marketplace changed for their products or how their work affected or didn't affect the company's rapidly changing challenges. They were almost as much in the dark as the GE workers of an earlier era.

Today, when so many work on an intellectual assembly line highly dependent on the smooth flow of information, line of sight is a critical concept. Each member of that assembly line needs to understand not only his or her work but how the accomplishment of that work affects the entire process and the resulting supply chain. And even that isn't enough. The understanding must also include the ultimate marketplace in which the product or service competes. What does the customer want and need? What are her alternatives to the product? Who are the competitors? How do they threaten that worker's livelihood and with what innovations? And given all of that, what is the company's business strategy to succeed in the marketplace?

Line of sight must also extend to the financial community and the demands and expectations of shareholders. How are those expectations and demands likely to affect the company's current and future prospects? And what of governmental bodies at the local, national, and even global level? What are their agendas and how will they affect the company's ability to do business?

All of these questions are the basis of the communication professional's need to build a sophisticated but simple story of the company's plight in a complex and chaotically changing world. In brief, the need is *to turn all employee eyes outward to the marketplace that determines success or failure* That need ups the ante for the communication professional to serve as an educator and storyteller rather than merely a purveyor of information. The marketplace becomes the ultimate source of the story and shapes the storyline about market forces and the company's strategy to deal with them effectively. Because the business strategy is always a set of responses to marketplace forces, the strategy must be positioned so as to make clear the connection to those forces. Only in that fashion can the need for worker line of sight be properly addressed and satisfied.

Context and Line of Sight

It's hard to fathom, but even today some senior leaders who believe in the doctrine of limited disclosure dispute the idea that line of sight is an important human need. They usually couch their objections in terms of concern over security of information and the alleged dangers of the competition finding out what the company is up to. Or worse, they voice the simple view that "people don't really need to know these things." I recall once presenting a strategic communication plan to a senior vice president of research and manufacturing, to improve his people's grasp of the marketplace, the business, and its needs. When I finished, he sat back, smiled patronizingly, and told me that all of this reminded him of the story of little Johnny asking his parents where he came from. The parents launch into an elaborate description of the birth process, only to be interrupted by Johnny protesting, "No, no . . . what I meant was that Bill told me that he came from Chicago. I wondered where *I* came from." For this senior VP, that joke closed the issue of what his people really needed or wanted to know at work.

The truth, in my experience, is quite the opposite. Employees tend to be aggressive information seekers in their desire to understand the business. I once asked a group of hourly workers where they got their most accurate information about the company. The conventional wisdom about hourly workers, even in companies that should know better, is that they are indifferent, mostly disengaged, and often not very bright. My experience gives the lie to that view. I find that more typically they are intelligent, anxious to understand the why's of the business, and willing but wary. One person responded to my question about his information-seeking: "I check the company website because they are more likely to tell the truth there, and then I get a copy of their mandated shareholder and Securities and Exchange reports from my broker and compare that information with what they're telling us in official messages on internal channels."

What is missing for most employees is the larger context in which their day-to-day experience is set. They often have lots of raw information; the challenge is putting that information into some sort of comprehensible context. Context is what line of sight is really all about. In the end, context derives from carefully crafted, simple, and memorable storytelling that links company strategy and initiatives to marketplace and customer demands.

In the 1990s Sears was in trouble as a result of new and aggressive competition from the likes of Wal-Mart and other nontraditional competitors. What had worked for years for the venerable supplier of everything from tools to washers to clothing was being threatened by cost-cutting rivals. A new CEO named Arthur Martinez decided to find ways to help employees quickly understand the company's plight and what had to be done about it.

He chose a simple and memorable phrase to convey what was required. He began telling employees everywhere he went that he wanted Sears to be "a compelling place"—a compelling place to shop, a compelling place to invest in, and a compelling place to work. In one simple phrase, repeated in all sorts of examples and guises, he captured a vision that would help employees cut through the distraction and noise and focus on results. More to the point, he was connecting the workplace with the marketplace.

Sears corporate communications then reinforced his educational effort with learning maps that graphically showed employees the path Sears had been traveling and engaged them in discussing what needed to be done to create that compelling place he envisioned. All of this repetition was critical to the Sears turnaround he led. What Martinez did so beautifully at Sears was to turn all eyes outward to the marketplace that was shaping Sears' business strategy.

Stickiness

Author Malcolm Gladwell was the first to introduce the concept of *stickiness*—the notion that certain ideas take on a life of their own and stick not only in our minds but also in the culture at large. In communication terms, stickiness is exactly what the word implies. It means stories, concepts, and messages that for one reason or another stay with people.

I'm reminded of the time when our five-year-old grandson, Joe, got to see his newborn twin cousins before his sister Sarah had the opportunity. My daughter knew that Sarah, who was a nine-year-old potential babysitter and a *girl*, would be upset about this evident breach of seniority. She warned Joe, in no uncertain terms, to keep his triumph to himself. That was a challenge for an excited five-year-old, but he later told me, bursting with satisfaction, that he had "kept that secret right in my brain." It was one of the best examples of a stickiness endorsement that I know of. The warning and even the logic of it had clearly stuck with him.

Chip and Dan Heath explain the stickiness concept further in their fascinating book *Made to Stick*. In their view, messages that stick share a certain set of predictable characteristics. They are simple, unexpected, concrete, credible, and emotional, and they are related in a story. If we apply those characteristics to the simple example of my grandson's dilemma, you can easily see what the authors are getting at. First, the message from Joe's mother to him was *simple*: "Whatever you do, don't tell your sister that you saw the twins before she did." It was *unexpected* in the sense that Joe was fully prepared to spill the beans until he was warned by his mother. Seeing the twins for the first time was also, for him, an unexpected and happy event.

Third, the message was about as *concrete* as it could be: *Keep your mouth shut.* No doubt about the meaning. Fourth, it was delivered by his mother, *the* most *credible* source possible in his young life. Fifth, there was clearly *emotion*. He was excited and thrilled by the experience, maybe less so by the negative emotion of the warning. In either case, it was memorable.

Finally, there was a *story* unfolding in his mind to help him remember and understand. He was with his grandparents, basically along for the ride when unexpectedly he got to see the newborn twins before his sister. He was fascinated with two tiny twin girls because he had only seen babies as single individuals; to see two who were almost identical was memorable. His first impulse was naturally to tell his sister and to describe the experience with a hint of triumph. But before he could see her and break the news, his mother intervened with a prohibition and a tone he understood clearly. No matter how tempting or exciting the prospect of topping his older sister was, he made the prudent decision to keep the message "stored in my brain," deciding instead to take pride in his ability to keep a secret no matter how difficult it was. Here was a heroic story he could one day recall and retell.

The Marketplace as Rationale for the Story

Now, aside from this simple and, for me, charming illustration, how do we apply the marketplace concept to effective communication with the workforce? To begin with, every company or organization has a marketplace story. It is always a human tale of a group of people engaged in a struggle to achieve a set of goals. Sometimes those goals are apparent, exciting, and worthy. Sometimes they are abstract or mundane in the overall scheme of life. But the struggle is always there, and understanding its nature is essential to satisfying people's need for a line of sight from their work to larger goals.

People at work require meaning and hope if they are to find satisfaction. So the purpose of the marketplace story is to supply the information that allows people to find that meaning and hope. That objective casts the communication professional in the critical role of educator and storyteller. It is a role that has been essential in human organizations since the beginning of time, a role that the elders of the tribe traditionally played. Families expanded the story by adding their particular histories and traditions to the larger history so that family members could understand not only how they fit in but also how important it was to be part of that story and of the tribal history.

In a very real sense that tradition is what contemporary communication professionals should be engaged in. It is their responsibility to help make sense of the human drama that takes place in every organization. All of us respond to stories. We are ourselves natural storytellers. Listen to people in recounting the everyday events of their lives. Most of those events, if they are memorable at all, will be told in the familiar form of a short story, with a beginning, a middle, a climax, and a conclusion. Stand at a gate at any airport and listen to the adventures of the passengers as they recount them to those waiting to greet them. If you have any doubts about our ability to inform and entertain one another with stories, those doubts will be erased by that simple experience.

Within organizations it's important for people to connect with the marketplace story if their work is to be more than a routine and monotonous day-to-day experience. No business strategy makes complete sense unless it's told in the context of the marketplace. Historically, we have been fairly proficient in telling the *what* in organizations: *Here is* what *we need to accomplish. We have made the following decisions. This is how we propose to proceed. We will keep you informed of results as we achieve them.* And so on.

Where we have been deficient is in telling the other half of the story—the more important half. *Here is* why *we are pursuing this particular strategy. This is* why *it is so important to our success. Here's* why *you should care, and here's* what *we expect of you if we are to achieve our collective goals.* It's the telling and retelling of the what *connected with the* why that makes the marketplace story and line of sight come alive.

I noted earlier that the task of performing an organization assessment is a lot like reading a novel. In doing the various interviews and listening to the views of the workforce, you hear the marketplace story unfolding before you. The goals become clearer because they are usually framed in why they are important to achieve. The challenges become clearer because they are portrayed with some degree of passion as well as confidence or anxiety about the outcomes.

The all-important vision becomes much more than the mere recital of a set of aspirations. It takes on the quality of a quest, a journey that is so important and inspiring that it is worth the pain that will be experienced along the way. The word *mission* and its suggestion of something important and vital in connection with the vision is not incidental. All of the members of the organization have their respective missions in pursuit of the vision. The true vision is expressed by visionaries with a sense of passion and excitement. And inspired missions are carried out by people with "*mission*ary zeal." That's the kind of stuff that gets people excited about their work when it is presented by a leader with a clear sense of what he or she is up to. Such leaders, by the way, don't necessarily have to be charismatic figures; they simply need to be perceived as sincere and knowledgeable.

If all of this is beginning to sound a bit rhapsodic and over-stated, consider how much of themselves people invest in their work. Think about the hours and the mind space they devote to that work. Think about what is at stake economically for all concerned if the venture succeeds or, alternatively, if it fails.

In listening to the workforce as you conduct your assessment, you also get a clear sense of people's desire to succeed as well as their sense of the obstacles that are put in their path by virtue of ill-considered decisions and policies. The frustration level is palpable as they argue for understanding and for a rationale they can use to comprehend the strategy and their roles in that strategy. The marketplace story, told simply and convincingly, arms them with a frame of reference that inoculates them against the otherwise chaotic nature of change and enables them to better cope with the inevitable setbacks and frustrations that they face in their work. If I understand the particular marketplace in which my organization operates, and if I see a clear connection between company strategy and marketplace imperatives, I am much more likely to be satisfied that the leadership has a solid strategy for success. All of that requires the communication professional to be a knowledgeable and accurate storyteller, able to assist leaders at all levels of the organization in shaping the story and saying, *This is why it is important. This is what we are striving to achieve together. This is the meaning of the otherwise abstract goals for our part of the business. And this is what you need to do to help us achieve them.*

The credible company is the one that can tell that story in such a way that an otherwise skeptical workforce will understand and, for the most part, embrace it. In practical terms, that means reducing the complexity of the marketplace and its loyal or fickle customers, with their needs and demands as well as their options, to understandable terms. It means cataloguing the various known competitors and talking about their strengths and vulnerabilities. It means identifying the market forces that shape the strategy and connecting the strategy to those forces. And it means resisting the tendency of organizations facing serious change to turn inward and to focus on their internal problems. In the end it means turning all eyes outward to the marketplace as the ultimate cause of the organization's marketplace story and strategy.

If there is a how-to formula for all of this, it comes down to identifying a handful of critical issues and crafting the honest and candid messages that make those issues crystal clear and meaningful. It also means creative repetition by all the organization's leadership voices (those that are official and credible and those that are unofficial and just as credible, if not more so) to the point where practically any employee can tell the story of what those issues mean to company success and to their own work.

In my view, this is what credible communication with otherwise skeptical workers is finally all about.

8

STRATEGY

Up to this point we have looked at a group of seemingly individual communication principles about information, employee needs on the job, face-to-face communication, openness, the necessity of careful employee research, and the importance of the marketplace in rationalizing and justifying work. It's now time to put them all together with the final letter of the INFORMS acronym, S—for *strategy*.

Internal communication strategy in the workplace is one of the most misunderstood and misapplied concepts in the profession. Both corporate leaders and their communication advisors tend to misunderstand what communication strategy is all about. Too often they confuse it with a simple set of communication tactics and channels aimed at organizational problems as they present themselves. The Chinese military strategist Sun Tzu, writing in 490 BC, had it right: "Strategy without tactics is the slowest route to victory. Tactics without strategy is the noise before defeat." Too many organizational communication efforts are literally the noise before the defeat of the effort.

Organizations depend on well-functioning systems that are guided by specific strategies, properly implemented and accountable. Communication is no exception. So the wonder is that in far too many companies, the communication effort is left to good intentions, to faith that information and news will move up and down the chain of command naturally, and to official reaction to one event or another.

Despite the superficial resemblances, internal communication is a far different animal from public communication. For one thing, employees have a heavily vested interest in the organization of which they are a part—much more so, obviously, than any casually interested party like customers or the general public. You may care about Company X if you use its products or services, but your level of caring is much less intense than that of the person who works for Company X. The employees' desire to know and understand their relationship and future in an organization is the motivation for their intense interest in whatever goes on in or affects that organization.

In far too many institutional organizations, communication is reactive, resembling the efforts of the news media: an event happens and everyone scrambles to tell what has happened in the most coherent terms possible. The early news is fragmentary and sometimes inaccurate. Rumors fill the air and exist in the same space as the official version, leaving the audience to make comparisons and speculate on causes and the motives of the principals. It generally takes some time for anyone to carry on an intelligent analysis of the news event and to put it into perspective for the audience.

All of that is a formula for disaster in organizations because it leads to misunderstanding, misinterpretation, and little attempt to explain *why* the event happened or the reasoning behind the decision now being announced. The problem is that too often the communication is not part of a strategy. Instead, it is a tactical resolution of a strategic problem.

Figure 8.1 shows the folly of that belief. It is a representation of what happens when the leaders convene over a given bit of news and then try to control its release internally.

Note that in the middle box in the left-hand column illustrating this scenario, the leadership group meets on Day 1 to consider an organizational event, an anticipated major action, or a decision they have made or will make jointly. Also on Day 1 two concurrent events take place. The first one, represented

Figure 8.1: The Typical Reactive Communication Process as It Works in Organizations.

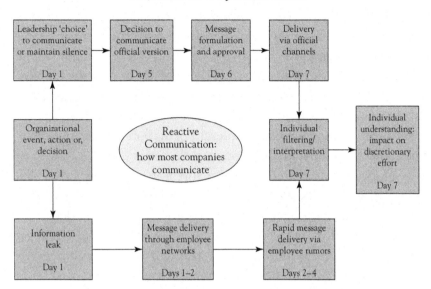

in the left box on the top line, is the leaders being faced with a choice to either communicate or maintain silence about the issue in question. This decision is usually one that they agonize over, particularly if the event is going to be regarded as bad news or in any way likely to generate a negative reaction. Too often, leaders decide to try to contain the information by remaining silent or refusing to comment further.

But the other event that also tends to take place on Day 1 is illustrated in the box in the lower left-hand corner. Someone in attendance at the meeting decides to tell a confidant what he or she has heard and swears them to silence. The trouble is, the confidant also has confidants in their respective networks, and the news begins to travel, each time with the admonition "Whatever you do, don't tell anyone else what I've just told you." Human nature being what it is, that is usually an invitation to do exactly the opposite.

These employee networks are notoriously leaky, so the news inevitably slips into the company rumor mill (see the box in the lower right-hand corner), with its propensity to enlarge, exaggerate, and fill in with imagined detail and speculation, so about all that is left is a headline with a story that is only a shadow of the original. For example, when I was with one company some years ago, the employee grapevine got wind of a retirement benefit that was soon to be announced. The trouble was that the employees added a few new wrinkles that were somewhat more generous than the actual plan. When what was a solid new company benefit was finally announced, the general population was deeply disappointed. The grapevine had concocted a better plan.

Notice what happens to the top line of the reactive diagram in Figure 8.1 when on Day 5 the leadership notices that the secret is no longer a secret. At that point they decide to tell their version, but it takes a day or so to formulate it and get it approved for release on Day 7 through official channels. By that time they are officially communicating "news" that is at least three days old and that has been widely shared by the informal channels. At that point the audience responds to whatever disparity exists between the official and the unofficial version and formulates a perception they add to all the other perceptions they hold about the leadership and its motives, trustworthiness, and likely future actions. Inevitably, those positive or negative perceptions have an impact on employee engagement and the willingness to expend discretionary effort.

Now add email, blogs, and other technology to the reactive process, and rev it up to warp speed so that the days represented here are compressed into hours and minutes, and you have a good idea of what's wrong with reactive communication.

So what's the alternative, in a wired world where information leaps national boundaries in a single bound and languages in an instant? The only answer that I know after all these years is to make internal communication strategic rather than tactical. That doesn't mean that one is the opposite of the other. It simply means that the tactics are part of a well-conceived strategy.

Keep in mind General Tzu's admonition: strategy without tactics is the slowest route to victory, while tactics without strategy result only in the noise before defeat. In modern terms that means that if we rely only on a set of tactics, no matter how efficient or fast they actually are, we are doomed to lose the communication race. The tactic of relying too heavily on instant communication technology, for example, only compounds the reactive process as leaders dither about what they can or can't say and wind up saying too little, too late, and the emails and blogs carry the messages that fill in the details, regardless of whether those details are accurate or not.

The Strategic Solution

The question naturally arises: how can you inoculate an employee population against the negative effects of reactive communication? The best answer is a robust communication strategy that works hard to create a rational line of sight for the employees. Let me set up a scenario of a fictional company and illustrate how such a strategy might be designed and executed. Although the company is fictional, it is based on a composite of several real companies and the kinds of problems they face in a global economy. The strategy is not a panacea, but it illustrates how the INFORMS principles can be applied in real circumstances. I'll attempt to tell the story with some of the challenges and roadblocks that I've seen in action through the years so that it is not a utopian solution fit only for idealized organizations with seemingly unlimited resources.

Here's our scenario:

- Derek Adams has been the CEO of Just In Time, Ltd. (JIT) for the last eighteen months.
- JIT was founded in Flint, Michigan, in 1929 as a supplier to the automotive industry there. It was renamed and

rebranded in 1983 after operating as Flint Auto Parts for most of its history.

- JIT employs twenty thousand people globally, with eight thousand in Flint, three thousand in Mexico, five thousand in China, and two thousand each in Germany and India.

- JIT revenue is $6 billion annually, with profits of $402 million. It is publicly held and listed on the NYSE.

- As a manufacturer, JIT prides itself on its strong value system and its progressive culture.

- Jennifer Murphy has been the director of internal communication at JIT for the last year. She was hired by Derek Adams and reports to the vice president of public affairs in Flint.

JIT Ltd. has experienced a rocky year, with revenues down by 2.4 percent from the prior year, although profits have increased to $402 million as a result of cost-cutting efforts. Derek Adams, the CEO, is generally well respected by both customers and employees, having come from General Motors, where he held a variety of executive positions in the United States and Asia. Under his leadership, profitability is up by a remarkable 37.5 percent increase over the prior year. Much of the increase has come at the expense of layoffs in Flint and in cutbacks in Germany and Mexico at the same time that employment in China and India has grown.

At Derek's urging, Jennifer Murphy has been looking for ways to improve employee understanding of the company's marketplace challenges and its recent actions to improve profitability. Because Derek's compensation is heavily incented with stock options and performance bonuses, he is strongly focused on company growth and profitability. But lately, with the layoffs and outsourcing of more and more work in both the United States and Europe, he is facing increasing employee dissatisfaction. In fact, the last employee survey conducted by Human Resources showed that trust levels in his leadership had eroded significantly.

Most of the write-in comments were directed at the issue of job insecurity in the United States and expressed concerns about increasing profitability at the expense of quality and increased investment in China, with its lower wage rates and less environmental concern or regulation.

When Jennifer was hired, she was struck by the primitive state of internal communication at JIT. There was an employee newsletter distributed monthly at the exits, with few takers. Most copies wound up in either the company wastebaskets or the company parking lot. Because of the manufacturing environment, with limited access to computers for many employees, most of the communication was conducted informally and face-to-face. Supervisors were not trained in their communication role, nor were they given much information or direction regarding that role. Derek and other members of his staff made an effort to conduct periodic employee town hall meetings, but they were hampered by the geography of the company, not to mention the issue of different time zones and cultures that limited communication opportunities.

Jennifer's sole prior communication experience was seven years in a high-tech company in Silicon Valley, where everyone had computer access and regularly logged on to the company intranet and other company information sources, including an executive blog with the opportunity for dialogue with all senior leaders, wikis for all interested participants to share information and views, a company equivalent of Facebook, and a culture in which employees referred to their BlackBerry devices as "CrackBerrys" because of their compulsive use by all hands.

When she first arrived at JIT, she had wondered how her experience would apply to this totally different culture. But Derek Adams had assured her that she had his full support in developing a communication strategy that would support his goal of increased employee understanding of the company's marketplace challenges.

After three months on the job, Jennifer decided that she really needed to understand where employee heads were at. She wanted to know whether they were a monolithic group or decided groupings within what everyone recognized—in Flint at least—as an older, high-seniority population on the verge of retirement. What information did they need? How and where did they want to receive it? Would one-size-fits-all communication work or were there underrepresented groups who needed special demographic attention? What were their views of the leadership? Did they trust them, after the changes that Adams had instituted? Did they understand *why* he was doing what he was doing? How about their supervisors? Did they recognize any sort of communication responsibilities? And was Adams really committed to being open and truthful with the workforce even when the news was distasteful? What was the level of understanding of the marketplace among employees? Did they recognize the global competitive threats that the company faced? How about the demands of the financial community for lower costs and increased profits? What did employees know about those demands, and what did they believe? And who were their most credible sources? Did they have any real contextual understanding of the business and their respective roles in it? These were the questions she needed answered if she was to do her job effectively.

She decided to begin her research by interviewing Derek Adams and his entire staff. The first interview with Derek went well. He repeated all of the things that he had been saying were the main elements of his leadership agenda and JIT business strategy. When she asked him about strategy, he recited some seven priorities that he had been emphasizing with all of his direct reports:

- Technological leadership in the industry
- Complete systems capabilities for JIT products
- Cost efficiency
- Excellence in product quality
- Global presence for JIT to better suit its customers
- The highest possible levels of customer service
- Dedicated, engaged, and motivated employees

He had been proclaiming these themes everywhere he went. He had also made them measures of success for each of his executives and had promised them that executive bonuses would be calibrated against their individual performance in achieving all seven strategic priorities.

In her next interview—with Herb Matthews, the VP of manufacturing—she was surprised to detect a bit of irritation in his replies. He had the longest tenure with JIT of any of the senior staff. After a few minutes, he paused, then asked quietly, "Look, is this off the record? Or are you going to quote me to Derek?" She assured him that all of the findings would be reported without attribution to any one interviewee.

He then confided to her that Derek talked a good game about product quality but that some of the tooling and machinery in the plant was badly out of date. It needed to be replaced, but every time he approached Derek about the need to invest in some new equipment, he was rebuffed out of hand. He added that the quality problems he was seeing in his reports were mostly a result of this refusal to modernize equipment. He finished with "You can't spin gold out of straw if the spinning wheel is defective." Other than this important lapse, he said, Adams was basically doing a good job.

Most of the other interviews showed that Derek's messages were getting through and were being pretty well heeded. The other exception to the rule was Mandi Andrews, the VP of human resources. After once more getting assurances that her comments were not for attribution, she told Jennifer her concerns regarding employee morale and lack of engagement among the Flint employees.

"Look, it's no secret that this town has been hard hit by the decline of the auto industry and that people are just glad to have jobs, but people are smart. They see the outsourcing and the investment in China and India, and they're worried. The good news for us is that the local workforce has nowhere else to go, but that's hardly a plus in getting people to feel engaged and good about the company or to recruit new talent with this aging workforce facing retirement."

The focus groups were, as expected, even more forthcoming and honest. "Look," said one supervisor, "how can I emphasize quality to these guys when they're doing their work on machines that should have been replaced five years ago? I don't have any answers for them when they tell me that that's the best they can do with this equipment. I've complained to Herb more times than I can count, and he's sick of hearing me. Last time he told me to stop whining and just get the work out. That's a helluva of a message to pass along."

In a focus group of the assembly line workers, the emotions were heated. "I don't trust Adams as far as I can throw him. He came in here with all of this talk about quality and costs, and the only thing he ever harps on is cost. Everyone knows that it's only a matter of time before he closes the Flint operations and takes everything to China. It's all a matter of labor costs. That's also why we don't get any new machinery and why our quality is not up to par. They're investing everything they can in China. I don't believe a word he says." When this worker finished, the rest of the group picked up on the theme like members of a jazz ensemble playing out their solo variations.

It turned out that the most credible source cited by the workers was the union leadership. The common view was that management told them the truth because they had to keep things running smoothly until the inevitable move of Flint operations to China, a fact that the union business agent never bothered to deny.

The diversity of the population was a bit of a surprise for Jennifer. She knew there was a small group of women engineers who had begun an informal series of meetings to discuss their mutual issues in a mostly male organization, but when she talked to a few of them she was surprised at the intensity of their feelings. They claimed that they didn't have the same opportunities for career development and promotion as the men did, and several of the most talented and specialized were talking seriously of leaving for a corporate culture more sensitive to their aspirations.

In terms of the diversity of the communications audience, she identified several more groups requiring some special attention and interest: the union leaders, a number of engineers recruited from the Middle East and India, and an ad hoc Black caucus.

In looking at the survey data from JIT's German operations in particular, Jennifer was struck by the continuing theme that U.S. leadership didn't understand the German corporate culture, let alone European views of subjects like trade unionism and the need to balance one's life in a small German town with the requirements of an increasingly demanding job. As far as any communication from JIT, the survey write-in comments showed that the workforce outside of the United States identified almost exclusively with their local operations and local leadership, not with some remote American company whose officials they had never seen.

When Jennifer had gathered all of the data together from ten interviews and a dozen focus groups, she sat in her office trying to figure out the real nature of her problem. She had Derek's promise of support, but she wondered if he had any idea how bad things were on the quality issues. Or if he knew how much local resentment there really was about the potential closing of Flint operations. How should she proceed? Should she hit him with the findings that showed him to be untrustworthy in the minds of the workforce? And to be only a name on a chart in operations outside the United States? How would he recover the lost trust? What could he do about operations that he was barely able to visit once or twice a year? And with only a newsletter that nobody bothered to take home and an implicit view that communication somehow just happened without much attention to strategy or to a disciplined system, how could she reach the workforce with the messages she believed they needed to understand?

She decided that she needed allies; that the findings—particularly those aimed personally at Adams—were too negative to deliver just on her own. Her first step was to go separately to Herb Matthews and Mandi Andrews, the two senior executives who had been honest enough to offer their misgivings about Derek's decisions and leadership style. When she sat with Herb, he surprised her again by telling her that most of the senior staff members were not on the same page with Adams. In their private discussions they had agreed that the quality issue was a matter of not investing in the machinery the plant required. But no one wanted to publicly support Herb because they had heard Adams flatly refuse to spend the capital that was required. The capital investment certainly was not a pure communication issue, Jennifer said, but it was having a dampening effect on all the rest of the CEO's messages, so it had to be surfaced.

When Jennifer spoke with Mandi, she was again surprised and reassured to learn that regardless of what the rumors were saying, there were absolutely no plans to move Flint operations to China. Mandi had prevailed on Derek on several occasions to make that clear, but his reply was that nothing was ever for sure in a global economy. He didn't want to make assurances that he might later have to take back.

When it was clear that Mandi and Herb had had numerous separate conversations about their respective concerns, Jennifer suggested to Mandi that the three of them form a united front and plan how best to deliver the research findings to Adams and the rest of the staff, along with a strategy to address the needs they had surfaced. Mandi quickly agreed, saying that this was the opportunity she had been looking for to pursue some of her own concerns. They then brought Herb Matthews into an offsite meeting to determine how to proceed.

In the end, the strategy that they designed together featured the following key elements. Herb resurrected the vendor proposals that he had solicited a year earlier and had the quotes updated. The accumulated quality reports for the last three quarters showed a slow but alarming dip in product quality as reported by JIT customers. Mandi dusted off a supervisory training proposal she had developed with an outside training firm, which she combined with the indications from the focus groups that employees were disillusioned with both their supervisors' inability to get results for their concerns and their inclination to overlook problem performers in their areas of operation. She then collaborated with Jennifer to design a communication awareness module for the supervisory training to drive home that particular responsibility. To put some teeth into the training, she designed a new communication leadership accountability for the performance management system, coupled with an inspection process in the company survey to ensure that individual supervisors and managers were taking their communication role seriously.

In the meantime, Mandi and Herb quietly began to speak separately with colleagues and to let them know that Jennifer was confirming some of their collective concerns with both anecdotal and survey data that all of them should be aware of. Adams had supported the data collection and said that he was anxious to see a final report of the findings. Mandi broke the news to him that there were some significant problems being surfaced and that Jennifer and she had been talking to determine what kind of joint strategy was necessary to begin addressing them. She made a particular point of surfacing the concerns of the female engineers and their ad hoc association as badly needing his sincere personal attention if JIT was to retain this important talent pool. She noted further that he needed to similarly direct some attention to the other diverse groups whose needs had been highlighted by the assessment.

Jennifer lobbied for a company intranet that was soon put into place to replace the unread newsletter and to carry important company news and events as well as to archive other company information. As she had identified middle managers, supervisors, and team leaders as important communication channels and as leading interpreters of company strategy and action, at Jennifer's request IT established a special intranet portal that could be accessed only by supervisors and managers with tools and information to aid their communication with their people.

After a private meeting in which the threesome briefed Adams on the employee concerns and the quality trend lines, he reluctantly agreed to make the necessary capital purchases and even to begin a blog that he would personally write, to be published both on the intranet and in print for all employees without computer access. The subject would be the marketplace challenges JIT faced and how those challenges continued to shape business strategy.

He decided to encourage computer access and greater computer literacy for all employees by offering a subsidized company purchase plan so that everyone would have a personal computer at his or her disposal at home, if not at work, with access to the intranet. Then, with Jennifer's help, he did something radical for JIT. He encouraged employees to reach out to one another and to form online groups based on common company concerns both in the United States and overseas. These groups in turn led to the development of wikis where collaboration was encouraged and where work teams invited their members to contribute their questions, concerns, and ideas about the projects they were involved in. He also agreed to meet with the women's group, give it official sanction, and work with them to address their issues.

Overall, Jennifer decided that the communication strategy she would undertake would be based on educating people in the marketplace realities and showing clearly how those realities shaped business strategy and imposed the need for change. She made the cogent point that practically every function in JIT in recent years had been forced to reinvent itself in reaction to the changes JIT faced. Communication, she noted, had to do the same thing and to make its efforts consistent with the demands of a contemporary organization in a tough competitive industry. To that end she worked with Adams and the senior staff to design a set of messages focused on the seven strategic priorities and to connect those priorities with real marketplace demands.

At the same time, using the quality issue and the refusal to invest capital in much-needed machinery as a prime example, she urged the leadership to make doubly sure that what they said matched their actions, so there was no say/do disagreement in their communications. She implored Adams in particular to explain himself more directly and openly so that people understood not only *what* he was doing but *why* he had decided to do it. She also thought that it was important to put to rest the rumors about closing Flint operations and moving the work to China.

But Adams steadfastly refused to announce that JIT operations would always remain in Flint, although he did keep everyone informed of the stakes of global competition and the issues that shaped JIT business strategy. He was careful to align that strategy with the issues and to make the alignment absolutely clear to all employees. Outside of Flint, he required the heads of operations in Mexico, Germany, China, and India to design a suitable communication initiative consistent with the respective needs and cultures of their operations. And he instituted a bonus system for them based on their business results and communication effectiveness as measured by employee surveys. If they didn't have satisfactory results, he warned, there would be no bonus.

He also personally committed to a series of television interviews that could be streamed through the company intranet once it was up and running properly so that he could better reach the diverse global population with his own views. And he directed his senior staff to become more active in their communication efforts with periodic and more frequent visits to global operations.

Was everyone happy and did employee satisfaction numbers soar? No. This composite fictionalized case was taken from the real world, with all of its complexities and contradictions. Some employees continued to mistrust Adams and his motives; others praised him for his efforts. Engagement levels increased somewhat, and supervisors tended to take their communication roles much more seriously, but more people complained of information overload and longed for the good old days when Chrysler, GM, and Ford had bought their products with limited competitive bidding and even less complaining about quality. And the job security issues among Flint employees remained as a continuing source of worry in a flat world.

But although the outcome of the new strategy was not a deliriously happy and satisfied workforce, they were certainly a better-informed workforce, which is probably the best outcome anyone can hope for in today's chaotic global economy.

What's the moral of Jennifer's story? It's simply the need to pay attention to the elements of the INFORMS acronym. Understand what *i*nformation people really need. Assess those *n*eeds based on standing research and the findings of your own observations and data gathering. Recognize that seemingly monolithic organizations are anything but, and that *f*ace-to-face communication is often required to further translate and reinforce the message. Push for greater *o*penness in what too often are secretive organizations in which even senior people don't talk openly to one another. Recognize that *r*esearch is necessary to tailor the message to the needs of diverse company groups. Try to improve employee lines of sight by educating them simply and concretely about *m*arketplace realities in a chaotic global economy. And, above all, be a *s*trategist who matches tactics to an overall set of goals and message priorities keyed to the marketplace—the ultimate source of and rationale for all organizational change.

And as for lessons learned? First, all organizations are superficially alike in a set of shared structural characteristics but vitally different in others, so what works in one place may well be a disaster in another. Also, communication is a complex leadership process that no one person owns or controls, because in the end it's all about individual perceptions. If you want to succeed with any communication strategy, you must be a collaborator with like-minded allies who contribute from their experience and knowledge to inform those perceptions as best they can. And, finally, be realistic in your expectations of success, which—contrary to common belief—is not "they lived happily ever after," but more like "they lived as well as they could with the knowledge that this is a complicated world where things don't always go your way, but at least you understand why things are the way they are."

Epilogue

A Profession at a Crossroads

"The employee audience in any large organization today is skeptical at best and cynical and turned off at worst. And they clearly have their reasons.

"This level of employee disenchantment was not always so . . ."

Those were my opening words in the Prologue. I've attempted to explain why the audience has grown skeptical over the years. Much of it can be traced to a world population living through mind-numbing change that has made people less trusting and more suspicious of leadership motives and actions.

There's obviously no turning back the clock on that history. For better or worse, we are what we are. The same is true of the workplace.

Those companies and other institutional organizations that have credibility problems with the people they employ have earned them mostly through either neglect or duplicity. Think about the nature of most institutional, profit-making organizations. Responding to Adam Smith's ancient theory of the Invisible Hand, they do what they do naturally and seek their own best interests in what most of their leaders tend to see as a dangerous and unfriendly world. Their evolution through the ages of a capitalistic society has left them with an essential—though not always a particularly appealing—identity that even the most enlightened of them share.

Suspend value judgments for a moment and consider the following facts of life. Business organizations are necessarily accountable and responsive to their owners' and shareholders' needs and demands. Their ultimate success depends on their performance in satisfying the fickle needs of their customers and beating their competitors in doing so. In a global world of pit-bull competition for customers who have almost infinite choices, this is no easy task.

In pursuing success, most organizations have resorted to a hierarchical and autocratic model because of its efficiency and clear lines of authority and accountability. That model has often led, unintentionally or otherwise, to bureaucratic practices and an emphasis on command and control, permission and approvals—not to mention a performance management system based on continuing personnel evaluation and attuned to the relatively primitive motivational process of reward and punishment. (Harry Levinson, in his classic book on human motivation, *The Great Jackass Fallacy,* asked rhetorically what you put between a carrot and a stick. His answer: a jackass.)

Because organizations see themselves first and foremost as private institutions living in an often unfriendly and threatening environment, they strongly resist government regulation of any kind and deeply resent public intrusion. Above all they respect performance, whatever measure they use to gauge that performance. For the most part they are conservative in their reaction to change unless they see a performance advantage in making changes to gain competitive advantage.

And as far as the people they employ, they cling unrelentingly to the doctrine of employment at will, which means that in practice everyone is on trial, with the jury always out on their performance. Because the owners and providers of the capital they depend on are usually not directly involved in the business, they employ a group of senior leaders and managers to oversee the operation, creating a class system in the organization, with power assigned to and jealously guarded by the most senior leaders.

That's the historical portrait of an American corporation that would resonate with most objective observers and employees—at least until contemporary times. It may sound a touch cynical, but in its broad outlines it is actually far more factual than cynical. For the most part the institutional organization lives by its own rules until and unless those rules come into conflict with the laws and values of a democratic society. In making and enforcing those rules the organization typically is not a democratic institution in the sense that everyone gets a vote. In George Orwell's immortal words in *Animal Farm*, "Some animals are more equal than others."

This lack of democracy and this tendency for corporations and other institutional organizations to pursue their own interests above the interests of outsiders have often created conflict between the organization and the larger society of which it is a part. And that conflict has created resentment, denunciations, and tensions that have colored American history for generations. The end product of all of this has been a degree of suspicion and a mutual lack of trust on the part of both the public and the corporation. Yet that lack of trust is mitigated by the recognition of mutual interest and dependence.

And here's the dilemma for the worker. He or she is both outsider and insider, customer and shareholder, private citizen and employee, antagonist and loyalist. What's more, he or she tends to share the mistrust of the public when it comes to private power. So it's a curious relationship, this business of being an appreciative and loyal employee on the one hand and an uneasy participant on the other.

In this sense at least, credibility and trust problems are inherent in the employment relationship. It has always been so.

A Power Shift

But as noted earlier, the nature of work and the profile of the worker have changed. He or she is no longer merely a cog in the assembly line. The worker is not merely a cost of doing business, as was the case for so long during the rise of the Industrial Revolution. Today's worker is the *means* of doing business. The worker's experience and education are the platform for the products and services the organization provides. So a natural power shift is taking place. It is now a relationship of greater dependence on the worker and that worker's unique skills and knowledge. At the same time workers are more dependent than ever on the timely and free flow of the accurate information they need to do their jobs and to collaborate with others in achieving organizational objectives. If nothing else, the workplace today is a collaborative enterprise with information as the primary raw material.

Today's workers are also much more sophisticated and demanding than their parents or grandparents were at work. In general they have been exposed to a much richer education and life experience. They have expectations—sometimes unrealistically so—of satisfying their career needs and finding personal fulfillment at work. They have less regard for power and for authority and chain-of-command rituals. And they also have at their disposal that great new leveler, electronic technology. As the printing press once challenged entrenched medieval authority, so the computer, in the hands of the contemporary worker, challenges entrenched corporate authority. Further, this is not just a phenomenon of western society. Third World or developing countries have awakened to the change and, equipped with the same aspirations, have access to the same technology universe. More to the point, their collective ambition and numbers are huge.

The Changing Role of Communication

All of the above have placed today's communication professional squarely at a crossroads that has great import for the profession and, more important, for the credibility of any company or other institutional organization. In greatly oversimplified terms, there are two important and defining issues. One is the matter of trust in formal and official communications. The other is the profession's growing love affair with mechanistic communication and the tendency to apply newer and newer technology as an end in itself, with slight regard to human needs in the workplace.

The trust issue comes down to this: who do you trust to give you reliable and candid information and to tell you the truth? Leaders with their own agenda and special interests, or your peers who seemingly have no agenda? Ironically, more and more communication professionals reply that their leaders have been guilty for some time of engaging in corporate speak—using corporate jargon and buzzwords and phrases to say little or nothing. They deplore the one-way, top-down, restricted flow of organizational communication and long for a model more in keeping with the dynamic networking nature of today's business organization.

In the view of the most disaffected communication professionals—a view that often strikes me as both schizophrenic and incredible, because they are a part of the traditional communication process they denigrate—the leadership cannot be trusted to tell the truth as they, the communication professionals and the organization's employees, see it. Rarely is it stated that baldly, but that is certainly the point now being presented by the disaffected.

The debate is a reflection of a fairly commonly held perspective in the blogosphere. To wit, authority always spins the truth and deliberately declines to provide honest facts and the full truth. By *authority* the critics mean just about all of the public media, the leaders of our institutions and, most of all, government officials and politicians. Now clearly there is enough obfuscation and spin provided by these sources to warrant a healthy degree of skepticism, but the opposite view now being promoted—that you can trust only communication from your peers and friends—is absurd. More to the point, it is a dangerous view in a democratic society.

That view has been inflated and perpetuated by the influence of countless blogs with what I call a "NeoComm" perspective on the issue of authority and power (that is, that it is always corrupted and corruptible). Here's an example of that influence on organizational communication, from a blog suggesting that face-to-face communication is vastly overrated and that its ultimate impact is to "*reinforce hierarchy* [italics mine] and deliver dumbed-down, one-size-fits-all messaging in organizations that actually work along networked lines."

That blog drew several opposing views; essentially, they made the point that face-to-face communication was a vital communication channel—albeit only one channel—for reaching a diverse employee population. But one of the responses was typical of the attitude I'm trying to capture. Speaking for a multitude of colleagues, the respondent noted, "Technology—and specifically Web 2.0 social media—are precisely the types of communication tools that foster the personal, straightforward, relevant, trusted communication that employees want . . . Do you trust CNN? The *NY Times?* Lou Dobbs? Or a friend who sent a micro blog while actually hearing Hillary Clinton or John McCain speak? . . . The same holds true inside companies—employees want the straight scoop and they'd prefer it from anyone they trust, not Corporate [sources]."

Now I have to say that if you accept the idea that the pronouncements of the establishment media are untrustworthy and if we extend that logic to company leaderships, we are left with only the option of talking to one another to get the "straight scoop." Inevitably that happens anyway, in one form or another, through our personal networks and through gossip. Any leader who demonstrates by her behavior that she's not to be trusted will soon find that the informal channels will carry the load for her instead. And, in fact, she will soon be in trouble as a credible information source.

Leaders, by definition, have the greatest access to the company information needed by the workforce to understand company direction and intention and to plan and manage their careers, whereas the informal channels rely on individual perception, shared confidences, rumor, overheard conversations, documents that happen to come across people's desks, and speculation about events, decisions, and leadership motives. Putting that puzzle together in a coherent, meaningful manner is almost impossible.

With the coming of a new generation to the workplace to replace those who are retiring, the Gen Y style of electronic communication may become irresistible. In a blink of an eye, the Internet has become a predominant communication force in our world. Similarly, company intranets have come to be *the* primary communication channel in most large organizations in the last few years. The result, in company after company, has been the demise of print publications for reasons of efficiency and cost. All sorts of electronic capabilities—like streaming video, real-time video conferencing to connect employees in different time zones and locations, as well as webinars in place of live training—have been added to the information mix. As a result, more and more communication depends on technology to increase the speed, effective contact, and, presumably, the productivity of the workforce.

It's hard to quarrel with this inclination to seek greater efficiency and speed in the communication process. But the open question is what this will ultimately do to the human spirit if we insist on increasingly mediating that process through digital devices that connect us only at a distant level but not really at a human level, a level and a place where we can touch one another physically and emotionally. Can the experience of constantly sitting in front of a computer or a projected image on a screen possibly be a satisfactory substitute for live human interaction? And what are the long-term social implications of such a workplace? It's a question worth pondering.

Evolution has made us social animals who need to connect at that human level if we are to be fully evolved human beings. Communication is, above all, an interaction with another human. It's conceivable that the virtual connection offered by technology will become the substitute for that kind of physical connection. Indeed, we could be entering a new era in human communication and relationships in which people are so enthralled and comfortable with electronic devices that they prefer virtual to real human contact. That exchange would come at a high price.

Professor Maryanne Wolf, a renowned reading and language expert at Tufts University, worries about what she calls "the addictive immediacy and overwhelming volume of information in the Googled world of digitally driven media."[10] She argues that such media offer "neither the time nor the motivation to think beyond the information given." In her view the sad result is that sophisticated thinking—including inference, critical analysis, and insight—is suffering. Again, it's a point worth pondering as we consider converting more and more communication to digital signals.

A Profession at the Crossroads

So what exactly is this crossroads of which I speak? It comes down to whether the profession will see technology as a seductive end rather than a remarkable means. It also comes down to whether the profession will see its role as being mere purveyors of information without regard to outcomes, to focus on craft at the expense of a balanced communication strategy. Craft is a tempting and easier alternative to the more difficult role of advocacy, education, and the greater humanizing of organizational practices and values.

What is at stake here is a complicated but rarely articulated debate about the real role of organizational communication in a complex and changing world. If you accept the unadorned profile of institutional organizations I cited earlier as typical, you see the nature of that emerging debate. The communication professionals, who argue that in our highly networked organizations the only communication model that you can trust is a horizontal as opposed to a vertical one, are guilty of perpetuating an either/or fallacy when in truth we need both types of models. To suggest that all or most leaders, as well as institutional pronouncements, are untrustworthy is not just wrongheaded; it is a self-defeating proposition for the profession.

What people at work continue to want is recognition for their contributions and for their individual worth and dignity as human beings. What they also need is credible information delivered by credible leaders who acknowledge their obligation to inform employees candidly about company direction and intention. They clearly reserve the right to be skeptical of those leaders when they have doubts, but they don't want them to be silenced or to not behave like leaders. Whatever the cause in our makeup, we look to official leaders with the expectation that they will lead us as rationally and as objectively as they know how.

We are undoubtedly in the throes of a revolution in the workplace from an industrial society to an information society. The changes are monumental and difficult for any one of us to understand completely. They are also, like so much of the change in our world, somewhat threatening and uncomfortable. We need *context* to help us weather the change. We need to understand how the external world affects our internal worlds. We need to understand the underlying reasons why, to help us cope. And we need a clear line of sight from our work to the overall needs and accomplishments of our organizations.

Some observers also argue urgently that we need communication professionals with the skills and insights to recognize and help solve communication blockages and information transmission problems in organizations—problems that limit our ability to collaborate and to manage the information assembly line efficiently. That will require a radical shift in the way communication professionals conceive of and perform their duties. It is unquestionably a vital issue and one that will require both a different orientation and a different focus in educating and managing communication staffs.

We also need institutional leaders with the courage to tell the truth as it happens and as they see it, to admit their own confusion in a complex world, and to listen intently to what their followers are saying about *their* needs and anxieties. We need local interpretation by people on the ground—managers, supervisors, and team leaders who understand local needs and who can translate how larger forces and events affect their work teams and what they must do to adjust.

In connection with all of that, we need to stop pretending that the admission of leadership misgiving and confusion will come as a surprise to the workforce. The nasty little secret is that they already know. They clearly understand that their leaders are not omniscient and that they make plenty of mistakes. What the workforce wants is an honest dialogue with flesh-and-blood leaders who are doing the best they can in a difficult set of circumstances. As Jack Welch put it so well some years ago when he headed General Electric, "If you're not confused today, you just don't understand the problem." In the end the workforce is infinitely generous in giving such leaders all the latitude and forbearance they require.

All of this will require much greater sophistication from communication professionals, who must understand as completely as possible the businesses and the marketplaces of which they are a part as well as the art and the craft they profess. Too often this is a profession distracted by novelty and searching for simple solutions to complicated communication problems.

To meet the challenges of today's world, practically every other corporate function has had to reinvent itself. Manufacturers learned lean manufacturing techniques and quality initiatives like Six Sigma to better cope with their companies' needs. They worked with vendors to provide just-in-time delivery and to create supply chain systems where they could assemble a product collaboratively with a variety of vendors. Engineers embraced a variety of technological tools to make their work more productive and to determine how better to collaborate in creating intellectual property. Sales people figured out how to find better ways to stay connected with customers and to satisfy their demands more quickly and more satisfactorily. And staff people have begun to recognize that they are more effective without the silo boundaries that have prevented collaboration in addressing complex organizational problems.

Now is the time for communication professionals to look for new ways to inform a skeptical audience and to work with their leadership to create the kind of understanding that will make the company credible in a changing world. Organizations are not going to change their fundamental nature: they are private enterprises pursuing a set of goals they perceive as inherent to their survival and self-interest and to the needs of customers and shareholders. What organizational leaders must change is their view that communication "just happens" in a well-run organization. Instead, they must recognize the need to make it a deliberate and accountable system, like all of the other systems and processes in the organization.

Some form and degree of autocracy is likely to be their chosen leadership style in what will probably continue to be power-laden structures, although the survival instinct will inevitably cause them to make modifications and to engage in considerably more power sharing. The world will continue to be both a threatening place and a vital global economy in which they will need to make changes, however uncomfortable they may feel about them—changes that communication professionals need to rationalize and communicate.

The Credible Company will be the one that recognizes all of this, applies the INFORMS principles to get through to that skeptical employee audience, and efficiently moves human energy in pursuit of worthy goals.

Notes

1. Institute for the Future and the Gallup Organization, "Managing Corporate Communications in the Information Age," 2000.
2. Survey on Workplace Communication (UK: Henley Management College, 2007).
3. Cited in C. Heath and D. Heath, *Made to Stick* (New York: Random House, 2007), 144–145.
4. M. Buckingham and C. Coffman, *First, Break All the Rules* (New York: Simon and Schuster, 1999), 30–34.
5. D. Sirota, I. Meltzer, and L. A. Mischkind, *The Enthusiastic Employee* (Upper Saddle River, NJ: Wharton School Publishing, 2005), 9–20.
6. C. Cozzani and J. L. Oakley, "Linking Organizational Characteristics to Employee Attitudes and Behavior," report of the Forum for People Performance Management and Measurement, Medill Integrated Marketing Communications (IMC), Northwestern University, 2000.
7. "Winning Strategies for a Global Workforce," a Towers Perrin HR Services Executive Report, 2005.
8. Buckingham and Coffman, 34.
9. T. L. Friedman, *The World Is Flat* (New York: Farrar, Straus and Giroux), 176–182.
10. M. Wolf, "Reading Minds," *The New Yorker*, January 28, 2008, 5.

Acknowledgments

After I wrote my last book, *Communicating for Change*, in 1996, I made a vow to myself not to do this again. It's a daunting process to write a book and to get it right. The problem is that time and change have a way of making an old book look like something you wore in the sixties, that era of fashion gone wrong.

I think every author must have that experience if they write over a period of years. This time I've taken a really audacious risk, because the world is spinning ever faster. What I say here may not stand the test of time. In fact, I will be surprised if it does, as fashions and circumstances change. To the extent that this book does pass the time test, I am indebted to my sponsoring editor, Kathe Sweeney at Jossey-Bass. Ernest Hemingway was once quoted as saying that good books are not written; they are rewritten. She challenged several important passages in the first draft and inspired me to rewrite them. That's what a good editor does. The result is a much more balanced effort than earlier drafts. Speaking of good editors, I owe a debt of gratitude to Kristi Hein, who labored over the manuscript and did an unbelievably thorough job in correcting my syntax and wrestling with my inferior knowledge of when to hyphenate or not hyphenate something.

I am also indebted to my friends and talented colleagues at ROI Communication in California, who were willing to indulge me as I dedicated my energies to this manuscript. I mention the leadership by name in the text because they are an inspiration in leading an open organization with a true focus not only on client communication but also on internal communication in their own company. Too often consultants are like shoemakers' shoeless children when it comes to company communication. Not so at ROI Communication, where all colleagues get a fair hearing for their ideas and concerns.

Unlike most of my generation, who were willing to settle into a company for forty years or so and retire, I have tended to follow my hopes and dreams and worked for a half dozen different organizations over the last fifty years. That's a long time to hang in, but as I've told anyone who has asked me why I didn't retire, "Why should I leave just when all of this got really exciting? I waited too long for that day."

Those organizations all taught me important lessons. Xerox Corporation, in particular, was a place where a young person was given lots of responsibility and the privilege of working with bright and talented colleagues. The failings that I cite in this book were more than compensated for by the attempts of senior executives like Joe Wilson, Peter McColough, and Dave Kearns to make the company a progressive organization that pursued excellence. It succeeded far more than it failed in that pursuit.

Similarly, Towers Perrin was for me a shining example of collaboration and excellence in consulting practices. My years there, as well as those at GE, Bell and Howell, and Mercer, were rich with the opportunity to learn and contribute.

My primary acknowledgment has to be reserved for my wife, my two daughters, and my two sons, who through the years have had to put up with all of this table talk about communication. I'm usually reluctant to show my work to others before I'm comfortable that it is my best. My daughters, Cynthia and Laura, who are also in the communication business, read the various versions of the manuscript and pronounced it as "great, your best work so far." That's the kind of affirmation that all uncertain authors, not to mention fathers, are looking for. My sons, Richard and Tony, were equally supportive and interested.

My sons-in-law, Mike Sweeney and Mark Cosmedy, and my daughters-in-law, Kathy and Anne D'Aprix, all expressed similar support and interest.

Finally, there is the long list of my professional colleagues and clients who have influenced my thinking about both communication and work. I trust that you know my debt to you, but I dare not mention you by name for fear of a memory lapse in omitting someone who made an important difference. I especially appreciate my friends at IABC and the Council of Communication Management who have taught me so much through the years. Ragan Communications should also come in for a special mention for their forbearance in allowing me to write a monthly column for *The Ragan Report*.

Thank you all for the pleasure of knowing and working with you.

The Author

Roger D'Aprix is an internationally known communication consultant, lecturer, and author who has assisted scores of Fortune 500 companies in developing their communication strategies and redesigning their communication training. His long list of clients includes such organizations as Comcast, Cisco Systems, DuPont, Lucent Technologies, General Motors, Saturn Corporation, Hewlett-Packard, EDS, GE Capital Services, Marsh, and scores of others.

In 1978 the International Association of Business Communicators honored D'Aprix as one of the youngest IABC Fellows ever named. That is the highest honor IABC gives. In 1998 IABC named him "one of the most influential thinkers in the communication profession in the last twenty-five years."

For fifteen years he held senior positions with two of the leading human resources consulting companies. He served as vice president and global practice leader for Towers Perrin's human resource communication practice and as principal and service developer for Mercer Human Resource Consulting. Before that, he was manager of employee communication for Xerox Corporation and held executive communication positions at General Electric and Bell and Howell.

Presently, he is vice president and advisory board member of ROI Communication, a Silicon Valley–based consultancy that specializes in internal communication consulting for large organizations.

He has written seven books on employee communication, including his best-selling *Communicating for Change: Connecting the Workplace with the Marketplace,* published by Jossey-Bass in 1996.

He is also a member of the advisory board of the UK publication *Strategic Communication Management* and a monthly columnist for *The Ragan Report.* A Phi Beta Kappa graduate of Hamilton College, he did his graduate work in psychology and counseling.

Index

A

Accessibility, 60
Accountability, 68–69
Animal Farm (Orwell), 137
Aspiration, 54
Assembly line, 19–20
Authority, 139

B

Baby boomers, 37
Baill, Barbara, 81
Baldridge Award, 5, 68
Best practices, 97–98
Billable hours, 21
Blogs, 33, 36. *See also* Social media
Bossidy, Larry, 87
Buckingham, Marcus, 46–48, 62–63
"Burning platform", 87–88

C

Carnegie Mellon, 29
Change communication, 8; and openness, 78–80. *See also* Communication
Communication: and business performance, 22–25; challenge of, 25–26;
changing role of, 138–142; and downsizing, 8–9; and employee engagement, 57–58; measurement, 102–104;
outputs and outcomes, 20–22; proactive, 30; reactive, 30; SOS strategy, 52;
trust in, 138, 139–140; typical reactive
communication process, 119; in Xerox
Corporation downsizing, 6–7. *See also*
Change communication; Face-to-face
communication; Information
Communication audit. *See* Organization
assessment

Communication professionals: at a
crossroads, 142–145; and face-to-face
communication, 70–71; and open-
ness, 75–76
Company call centers, 21
Context, and line of sight, 109–110
Contributions, recognition for, 44
Corporate democracy, and social media,
34–37
Covey, Stephen R., 31–32
The Cult of the Amateur (Keen), 36

D

Data gathering, 88–89. *See also* Research
Downsizing, 2; and communication, 8–9,
79–80; long-term costs of, 7. *See also*
Layoffs

E

Electronic communication. *See*
Technology
Employee engagement, 43, 53–56; and
communication, 57–58; possible
level of, 56–57; study at Gallup
Organization, 46–48. *See also*
Participative management
Employee satisfaction, 48–51
Executive interviews, 89–90; typical
interview questions, 90–92

F

Face-to-face communication, 11–12,
47–48; accessibility, 60–61; accountability, 68–69; augmenting high tech
with high touch, 69–70; frontline communication, 62–67; and the professional communicator, 70–71; tools, 69;

Face-to-face communication (*continued*) training, 68, 69; what it looks like, 59–60. *See also* Communication
Fagan-Smith, Barbara, 81–82
FedEx Express, communication initiative, 24
First, Break All the Rules (Buckingham), 46, 62–63
Focus groups, 92; agenda, 96–97; guidelines, 92–95
Ford, Henry, 19
Friedman, Thomas, 105–106

G

Gallup Organization, employee engagement study, 46–48
General Electric (GE), 144; Light Military Electronics Department, 107
General Motors, 107
Generation X, 37
Generation Y, 35, 37–41
Gladwell, Malcolm, 110
Gommersall, Earl, 43–46, 56
The Great Jackass Fallacy (Levinson), 136

H

Heath, Chip, 111
Heath, Dan, 111
Henley College, 28

I

Ignorance, three levels of, 80–81
Immelt, Jeffrey, 40–41
Information, 10–11; accuracy, 20–21; and business performance, 22–25; challenge of, 25–26; completeness, 21; consequences of technology, 26–29; democracy, 32–34; mixed messages, 21, 22; technology and role definition, 29–32; timeliness, 20. *See also* Communication
Information purveyors, 17–18
Information society, 18
INFORMS acronym, 14–15
Inspiration, 54
Institute for the Future, 28
Intellectual capital, 19–20
Internal communication, 74–75; typical reactive communication process, 119. *See also* Communication
Invisible Hand theory, 135

J

Job mastery, 44, 49
Just In Time, Ltd. (JIT) fictional scenario, 121–133

K

Kearns, Dave, 2–5
Keen, Andrew, 36

L

Layoffs: and communication, 8–9; long-term costs of, 7; Xerox Corporation, 1–5
Leadership, 22
Levinson, Harry, 136
Lewis, Sheryl, 81
Line of sight: and context, 109–110; from vertical to horizontal, 106–108

M

Made to Stick (Heath and Heath), 111
Marketplace, 90; context and line of sight, 109–110; as rationale for the story, 112–115; stickiness, 110–112; triple convergence, 105–106; from vertical to horizontal line of sight, 106–108; and workplace, 13
Martinez, Arthur, 110
Medill Integrated Marketing Communications (IMC) graduate program, employee satisfaction study, 51
Message boards, 34. *See also* Social media
Millennials, 38. *See also* Generation Y
Morale, 48

N

Nadler, David, 5
Needs of the audience, 11, 43; determining needs in your organization, 52–53; employee satisfaction, 48–51; employee's communication needs on the job, 66; Gallup Organization study, 46–48; Texas Instruments study, 43–46. *See also* Employee engagement

O

Open-Book Management, 80–81
Openness, 12, 73–76; and change communication, 78–80; examples, 80–85;

inevitability of, 85; need-to-know doctrine, 76–78; three levels of ignorance, 80–81

Organization assessment: developing the plan, 99–100; executive interviews, 89–90; map of, 89; presenting findings, 98–99; typical interview questions, 90–92. *See also* Research

Orwell, George, 137

P

Participative management, study at Texas Instruments, 43–46

Perdue, Frank, 61–62

Perdue Farms, 61–62

Pitney Bowes, 28

Potter, Les, 37–38

Power shift, 137–138

Predictability, 44

Proactive communication, 30

Procter & Gamble, 34

Prophets in the Dark (Kearns and Nadler), 5

Q

Quirke, Bill, 52

R

Reactive communication, 30; strategic solution, 121–133; typical reactive communication process, 119. *See also* Communication

Reed, Stu, 103

Research, 12–13; best practices, 97–98; data gathering, 88–89; executive interviews, 89–90; focus groups, 92–97; measurement of results, 102–104; presenting findings, 98–99; quantitative vs. qualitative, 100–101; translating into a plan, 99–100

ROI Communication, 81–82; Executive Communication Forum, 103–104

Role definition, 29–32

S

Sears, 110

Shaffer, Jim, 22–23, 24, 61–62

Sirota, David, 48–49

Smith, Adam, 135

Social media: and corporate democracy, 34–37; and information democracy, 32–34

SOS strategy, 52

Spaulding, George, 61

SRC Holding Corporation, 80

Stack, Jack, 80–81

Stickiness, 110–112

Strategic Communication Management, 36

Strategy, 13–14, 117–121; strategic solution to reactive communication, 121–133; and tactics, 121

Surveys, 100–101

T

Tactics, and strategy, 121

Technology, 18, 41; as an end in itself, 138, 141; information and role definition, 29–32; information consequences of, 26–29; and information democracy, 32–34; studies of technology and information overload, 27–29. *See also* Social media

Texas Instruments, participative management study, 43–46, 56

Tools, 69

Towers Perrin: employee engagement study, 53–56, 57; Perdue Farms, 61–62

Training, 68, 69

Transparency, 73–74. *See also* Openness

Triple convergence, 105–106

Trust, 138, 139–140

Tzu, Sun, 117, 121

W

Welch, Jack, 144

Wikis, 33–34. *See also* Social media

Winslow, Frederick, 19

Wolf, Maryanne, 142

Workers, changing profile of, 137–138

Workplace, and marketplace, 13

X

Xerox Corporation: full employment policy, 1; layoffs/downsizing, 1–5; Leadership Through Quality initiative, 68; manager effectiveness survey, 61